Common Diseases of the Fancy Rat

NFRS Handbook – Part One

Written and compiled by

ANN STOREY MSc, FIBMS

National Fancy Rat Society

Published by the National Fancy Rat Society
PO Box 24207, London SE9 5ZF

© National Fancy Rat Society 2007

ISBN 0-9554025-0-6

ERRATA

PAGE 14. THE DRUG GIVEN FOR THE TREATMENT OF
EPILEPSY IS INCORRECT. IT SHOULD BE SODIUM
PHENOBARBITONE AND NOT PENTABARBITOL.

Contents

1 INTRODUCTION – CARE OF THE SICK RAT

I must start this by saying that ill health should not be the normal state for your rat, although you would certainly think it was whenever you open a copy of *Pro-rat-a*, the journal of the National Fancy Rat Society, or any internet forum. Provided that your rats have been bred for good health, properly looked after, kept in a clean, well aired environment, fed properly, not allowed to become too fat and not allowed to rear litters too often or when they are too young or too old; your animals should rarely suffer serious illness. I am constantly amazed at some people who seem to spend a fortune on veterinary bills when the money would be better spent on improved husbandry. It must be said that there is a difference between the person keeping a few pets and the person considered to be a stock breeder.

Most pet-keepers do not keep large numbers of rats and are less likely to suffer from the epidemics a fancier's rats are prone to, but because the rats normally live out their full lives of between two and three years, many will fall prey to the diseases of ageing, such as chronic respiratory disease, tumours, arthritis, kidney disease and so on. Here it must be remembered that while many of these conditions can be controlled, eventually there will come a time when the rat no longer finds living a pleasure. It is then much better to have him painlessly destroyed than to let him suffer.

Many fanciers, on the other hand, are less likely to treat an animal if it is unlikely to make a good recovery, its performance in the breeding pen is affected or if it is putting the rest of the stock at risk. An epidemic disease in a stud can wreak havoc, especially if it also spreads to other animals at a show.

The bottom line is to follow the precepts of the Hippocratic oath to 'Do no harm' and to prevent suffering by whatever means is most appropriate to the circumstances.

1.1 Spotting the symptoms

It is important to be able to recognise when your rat is off colour so that appropriate steps can be taken. Any of the following may indicate trouble: staring coat, hunched appearance, diarrhoea, wet vent, sores and scabs, reddened or dry areas of skin, coat loss, sneezing, discharge from eyes, ears or nose, lumps, weight loss and blue tinged extremities. Pain can be difficult to spot in a rat as they tend to hide it because other rats may take it as a sign of weakness.

Symptoms of pain include sunken eyes and an inward look, staring coat, sitting hunched up, flattened ears and a disinclination to move or sometimes eat. In a hutch you may find that they will sit facing a corner away from the entrance. In a wire cage with a nest box, they may refuse to come out. Remember, you are the expert on your own rat. Watch him so that you know what normal behaviour is and when something might be going wrong. Smell is also important. Is there a different smell associated with him? A foul smell may indicate intestinal disease or a wound infection and a smell of pear drops, boiled sugar or lager may indicate a metabolic disease such as diabetes. Hearing, listen to his breathing, is it noisier than usual? Touch, does he feel lighter or more fragile than usual? Can you feel any lumps or anything unusual? Any of these signs may indicate that something is not quite right.

1.2 Nursing care

When illness is suspected, decide quickly if it is a condition you can treat yourself, the rat needs a vet or the rat should be put down. Some conditions are incurable and very unpleasant for the animal, in which case it should quickly be put down and not put through the trauma of pointless treatment.

If you decide to treat, it must be remembered that it is not good enough to just push a few drugs down its throat two or three times a day. A sick rat will require nursing. For a start make sure that the rat is comfortably bedded down on some soft absorbent bedding. A layer of hay or tissue paper on top of shavings or other bedding is fine; otherwise a piece of Vetbed is very good. This can be washed and reused many times. The cage should be placed in a warm, draught free place but still with plenty of air. If the rat is off its feet, especially if it has a respiratory complaint, you will have to turn it over every two or three hours to prevent it getting pneumonia. If they are cold, a hot water bottle wrapped in a towel, a heat lamp or a heat pad such as those sold for reptiles can be used. Make sure that some of the cage is unheated though, so that the rat can get away from it if necessary. However, if the rat is not moving much you should then watch carefully to make sure that it does not become overheated. You can tell this by checking that the ears do not become too red. Do not leave an unconscious rat on a heat source unattended for more than a few minutes and make sure it is used according to instructions.

Dehydration can be a problem, so make sure that plenty of liquids are consumed. The rehydration fluids available from the chemist such as Dioralyte are good for this but you can make your own using five or six teaspoons of glucose and one of salt in a litre of water. Alternatively your vet can supply you with a product such as Lectade. It is not necessary to use boiled water to make up any of these solutions. Dehydration is a big killer in rats with diarrhoea and pneumonia but it is easy to diagnose. Normally, if you gently pinch an area of the rat's skin, the area of pinched up skin quickly springs back to normal. If a rat is dehydrated the skin does not return to normal but lacks elasticity and stays where it is. If you are sure that the rat is not dehydrated, you can feed it any of the products sold for sick and convalescent animals as well. You may have to use a medicine dropper, syringe or kitten feeding bottle to give fluids if the rat is not drinking much. Push the dropper into the corner of the rat's mouth, angling it towards the back, squeeze gently to allow some fluid out but not enough to drown the rat! You will probably need to repeat this every two hours. It is better to get 0.5ml in regularly than 5ml in every six hours. For unconscious rats injections under the skin with sterile fluids should be considered. Depending on the size of the rat it is possible to give 5ml of fluid per site using this method. Your vet can advise you on this.

If the rat has diarrhoea or any other discharge and is unable to clear it up for itself, you must do it for it using baby wipes or moist cotton wool. Remember that sick rats that are in pain or having trouble breathing may bite when they are picked up. Various methods of restraint are given in *Rat Health Care* by Debbie Ducommun. However, it is a good idea to practise these on fit rats so that you become proficient before you have to use them on a sick one. In my experience the best method is to get another rat orientated person to hold the rat for you. It is best not to use gloves as these reduce mobility (for the operator!) and can frighten the rat.

If the rat starts to recover you should encourage him to eat by giving him something tempting such as porridge or custard or convalescent food sold for sick animals.

1.3 Infectious disease

When infection is suspected, you should isolate the affected rat and its cagemates. This means keeping them in a separate room and thoroughly washing your hands before you handle the rest of your stock. Sick rats should not come in contact with your clothes or hair unless you wish to wash these before handling other rats. Ideally you should wear protective clothing and a hair covering. Remember that a few infectious rat diseases can be transmitted to humans. Therefore always remember to wash your hands and report any unusual symptoms in yourself to your GP. It is unwise to let children play with sick rats.

For breeders, if you suspect an outbreak of infectious disease it is unwise to show during this period. Neither should you sell any rats or send them for export. When you send rats for export you are normally requested to sign a document indicating that your stock is free from symptoms of infectious disease. To deliberately lie about this is both illegal and contrary to the spirit of good sportsmanship. You should leave three weeks after the last case.

You may decide that culling the infected rats is better. However, some infectious diseases are so infectious that culling or quarantining infected rats is too late. To try to avoid problems it is advisable to quarantine new rats or rats that have been shown for about two to three weeks. Do not mate up rats directly they have come home from a show but leave them for the quarantine period. It has to be said however that not all animals infected with a disease will show symptoms and some diseases have an incubation period of more than three weeks. Therefore, just because a rat has been quarantined does not rule out the possibility of it still being a source of infection. To quarantine rats, they should be kept in a separate room or building and you should not visit your other rats immediately after the quarantined rats. You must keep a change of clothes and shoes for visiting the quarantinees and preferably shower as well. Therefore it is best to visit these rats last thing at night, in order to cut down on work. However most people who show do not really quarantine their stock and it has to be said that if you are going to attend shows with your rats it is inevitable that they will sometimes pick up infection. Some infections, such as respiratory viruses, are so common that you may consider it better that you allow all your rats to become infected in order that a degree of immunity can be attained. This is a personal decision. 'Vetting in' or other policies carried out in order to prevent the spread of infection at shows do not detect those carrier rats with no or slight symptoms. The use of antiseptic wipes by judges is not much more than a cosmetic exercise. These are not effective against all groups of pathogens, don't protect against airborne pathogens and are not effective the way they are used. However, judges should wash their hands after handling rats they suspect of being ill.

Imported rats are a different proposition. In this case the owner should maintain a good quarantine regimen until they are sure that the animals are healthy.

1.4 Accidents

Obviously it is better to avoid accidents but these do happen, especially to free range rats. The most common are listed below.

1.4.1 Falls or crushing

Check for broken bones (see paragraph 3.11.1), swellings or bleeding, either from cuts or from any orifice. If you suspect serious injury or the rat is stunned or in pain, it is advisable to take the rat to the vet. If the rat appears shocked try sugar and water or Bach's Rescue remedy. Keep the patient warm and quiet. Try Arnica homoeopathic remedy.

Shelves or other high-rise equipment in tall cages can cause problems for larger or older rats. I have had several people report breaks, sprains and tail root injuries in large rats who have landed badly after leaping from a shelf. Therefore I would advise that a maximum shelf height for adult males of 60cm is recommended. It is not enough to provide them with a ladder. Rats are not squirrels and high cages are not necessary. You can make a perfectly interesting cage without resorting to a trapeze act!

1.4.2 Bites and abscesses see paragraph 3.9.7

1.4.3 Broken teeth see paragraph 3.2.4

1.4.4 Skinned tail see paragraph 3.10.4

1.4.5 Burns and scalds

Apply ice (ice cube bags are good) or cold water. Seek veterinary advice. These can be very serious in rats due to dehydration and the risk of infection. Do not apply ice for more than five minutes at a time in case you cause frost bite.

1.4.6 Poison consumption including house plants, drugs, cleaning fluid etc

Do not attempt to induce vomiting as rats are unable to do this. Seek veterinary advice as soon as possible remembering to take the product, plant name etc with you. Try giving water or milk to drink.

2 DRUG TREATMENTS

Drugs, if used, must be given regularly and in the correct dosage. The rat must always finish the course unless the vet has advised otherwise, they are making the rat worse or they are plainly having no effect (remembering to give the drug a reasonable amount of time). It is better not to give medicine in the drinking water as it may put the rat off drinking. If available use a palatable formulation that the rat is happy to take as it is. Otherwise you can try combining it in food that the rat likes. Jam is quite good. Do not combine tetracyclines with dairy products as these can inactivate this class of drugs. It is important to remember that not all drugs are passed for use in all species, and not all drugs are equally useful or safe in all species. For instance, it is perfectly safe to give rats penicillin but not cavies. Therefore a vet may refuse to prescribe a certain drug in such cases. Fanciers, who may require treatment for a lot of rats on occasions, should get to know a vet well first. Do not roll up to the surgery asking a strange vet for X amount of drug to treat Y amount of rats as they are quite likely (and rightly) to refuse. A good relationship with your vet is more likely to mean that they will show you how to inject and other skills thus saving you lots of money. If you are a breeder then it is important to try to find a vet who is sympathetic or at least tolerant of your aims. Some aren't and seeing the animals turned out by some animal breeders you can't really blame them.

2.1 Conventional treatments

Here follows a list of drugs which have been used and their approximate doses, but as there is a certain amount of disagreement about dosing, your vet may suggest different quantities. Determining dosage for small mammals by extrapolating from large animal or human data is a very blunt instrument. It is important not just to take into account the size and surface area of the species concerned but also the relative differences in metabolic rate. There are frequently differences in the way species metabolise and excrete drugs as well.

These doses come from more than one source and I have concentrated on oral or subcutaneous treatments which an owner may be able to give for themselves. Remember, all drugs (including herbal and other 'alternative' preparations) may carry side effects. If these occur, then providing the drugs have been properly prescribed and used, this is not the fault of the vet or anyone else, it is just bad luck, although the vet should make you aware of any risks.

2.1.1 Antibiotics

Do not overuse these, as resistance, not only in the bacteria you are treating but in any other bacteria in contact with the drug, is a real problem. Antibiotics may cause

Abbreviations used in tables on the following pages
BID – twice daily
TID – three times daily
sc – subcutaneously (under the skin)
im – intramuscularly
topical – for use on the skin, eyes, ears etc
All doses are given as weight of drug per weight of animal (mg/kg etc) unless otherwise stated

diarrhoea. If your rat develops diarrhoea while on antibiotics, consult your vet immediately. Antibiotic associated diarrhoea is rare in the rat but common in hamsters and cavies, where it is quite often fatal.

Some vets like to give antibiotics post-operatively to prevent infection. However, the evidence shows that the antibiotics are much more effective if given *before* the operation, so that good blood levels are there when the bacteria are introduced into the blood stream.

Antibiotics

Product	Dosage
Synulox (amoxycillin, ampicillin is virtually the same antibiotic)	Between 25-150mg/kg by mouth or sc, depending on author
Amoxycillin + clavulanic acid	14mg/kg by mouth
Cephalexin	60mg/kg orally, once per day
Chloramphenicol (Chloromycetin)	20-50mg/kg orally BID or topical eye ointment etc
Gentamicin	4.4mg/kg im or sc BID. Do not overdose, can be toxic to kidneys and ears, encourage drinking. Also available as topical ointment
Benzylpenicillin	20,000units/kg orally once per day
Neomycin	50mg/kg orally once per day or 2g/l in drinking water. Available as drops. Some topical preparations contain steroids and antifungals
Oxytetracycline	60mg/kg orally once per day but may not reach useful concentrations in the blood. Do not use on pregnant or nursing does or rats under three months
Tetracycline	20mg/kg orally BID. Do not use on pregnant or nursing does or rats under three months. Also available as ointment
Doxycycline	5mg/kg orally BID. Do not use on pregnant or nursing does or rats under three months
Baytril (enrofloxacin)	5-10mg/kg orally BID. Do not use on pregnant or nursing does, rats under three months or rats with kidney disease. Best reserved for serious infections. The higher dose is recommended by most rat researchers including the University of California
Erythromycin	20mg/kg orally TID
Metronidazole	For Tyzzer's disease and antibiotic associated colitis. Added to drinking water at a rate of 2.5mg/ml
Borgal (trimethoprim/sulphadoxine)	0.5ml/kg daily sc
Tribrissen or Septrin (trimethoprim/sulphadiazine)	30mg/kg orally BID

2.1.2 Antifungals

Product	Dosage
Griseofulvin	25-50mg/kg orally BID (at least 14-60 days)
Ketoconazole	10-40mg/kg orally per day (14 days). Topical preparations are also effective

2.1.3 Antiparasitics

Product	Dosage and use
Droncit (praziquantel)	6-10mg/kg orally, repeated in 10 days for tapeworm
Ivomec/Oromec (ivermectin)	0.2-0.4mg/kg orally every 7-10 days, or, 1% ivermectin diluted 1:100 with 1:1 propylene glycol: water (or corn oil) placed on or behind the ears for mites and lice. For pinworms 25 mg/l drinking water on days 1-4, 8-11, 15-18, 22-25. For bladder worms, 3mg/kg by mouth (once)
Panacur (fenbendazole)	0.5ml/kg (50mg/kg) for three days. For all roundworms including bladderworms. Also 150mg/kg of feed on weeks 1 and 3 for 3 weeks for pinworms
Johnson's Kitten Wormer (piperazine citrate)	10mg/ml in water for 7 days on/7 days off/7 days on. For all roundworms but not as effective as Panacur
Frontline (fipronil)	7.5mg/kg. The commercial spray is rather strong to use undiluted on rats. Do not repeat more than once per month
Johnson's Antimite Spray (pyrethrin)	Light spray repeated weekly. Avoid spraying the face. Reported to cause allergic responses. If a rat has trouble breathing after administration seek veterinary advice
Vapona (dichlorvos)	Commercial strips hung in rat room. Good for controlling ectoparasites such as lice and mites. Said to cause infertility in does but used without problems by many fanciers for years. Difficult to obtain

2.1.4 Analgesia

Product	Dosage and use
Buprenorphine	0.01-0.05mg/kg sc every 8-12 hrs. Excellent post operative pain killer. Flecknell recommends a single dose following minor surgery (mammary tumour removal etc) and treatment for 36 hours plus for more serious surgery
Buscopan (hyoscine)	Antispasmodic and analgesic for gastrointestinal disorders and colic. For adults either 0.2ml sc BID or 1/4 10g tablet BID
Paracetamol (use Calpol Sixplus meant for children)	100-300mg/kg every 4 hours. If you use Calpol Sixplus a 500 g rat will need 1-3 ml. This will also reduce fever
Aspirin (use Asproclear in drinking water)	100mg/kg every 4 hours. Two tablets of dispersible aspirin in 500ml water is satisfactory. Good anti-inflammatory but is said to cause birth defects in rats. Therefore do not use on pregnant does
Metacam (meloxicam)	Available in a 10ml dropper bottle. 4 drops/kg (0.2ml/kg) for acute pain and 2 drops (0.1ml) for chronic pain mixed with food. Anti-inflammatory, antipyretic, analgesic. Not for use under 6 weeks
Ibuprofen	10-30mg/kg every four hours. For post-operative pain relief 280mg/kg/day by mouth 1 hour before surgery then 70mg/kg 8-12 hours after surgery. Good anti-inflammatory. Probably more effective pain killer than paracetamol and aspirin. Available from pharmacies as a syrup for children. A 500g rat can be given 1-2 ml three times a day

Some vets like to give analgesics preoperatively. These usually wear off within 24 hours but this is usually enough time for any post-operative pain to diminish to the point where the rat is able to function more or less normally. Rats suffering considerable post-operative pain or where the sutures are causing discomfort are more likely to worry the wound than those that feel comfortable.

2.1.5 Anaesthetics

It is generally considered that the best anaesthetic for use on rats is the gaseous anaesthetic isoflurane. This is because the recovery time is quicker and it is less toxic to the liver than halothane, which is also widely used. Other anaesthetic gases are available. If you intend to have surgery performed on your rats it is advisable that you first check which anaesthetic method they use on rats when making your choice of veterinary practice. Halothane may occasionally induce overheating in some rats. This condition can be controlled if spotted in time. The trouble is that most of the time the problem is hypothermia or loss of body heat, meaning that it is good practice to use heat lamps or pads on anaesthetised rats. While they are recovering rats should be watched constantly for both conditions. Overheating rats first develop red ears. In laboratories, where the injectable anaesthetic pentobarbital is used I have also seen rats develop overheating. Injectable anaesthetics are not recommended for pet rats because of possible complications caused by underlying respiratory disease.

2.1.6 Miscellaneous

Product	Dosage and use
Bisolvon (bromhexane)	Decongestant. Powder formulation 10mg sachets. A dosage of 1mg/kg recommended by NFRS member, Claire Jordan
Valium (diazepam)	Sedative - 5mg/kg for tooth trimming or other techniques which may upset the rat
Olbas oil/Vick/eucalyptus oil	Used for improving breathing in respiratory disease. Place some on tissues or cotton wool in a small jam jar. Put the lid on and puncture the lid in several places. This will let the vapours out but keep the rat from eating the preparation
Pepto-Bismol/Kaopectate etc	For diarrhoea. Various paediatric preparations available. Approx 0.5ml orally TID
Tamoxifen	1mg/kg orally daily. Debbie Ducommun recommends 1mg/rat daily. Some rats dislike the taste and so as this has to be used on the long term, this may affect success. For the treatment of mammary fibroadenomas, experimental
Oxytocin	0.1-3.0units/kg sc or im. For delayed parturition especially uterine inertia (cervix must be dilated) and where the doe is not producing milk (agalactia)
Pseudoephedrine	Nasal decongestant. May be useful for treating acute respiratory symptoms. Use paediatric cough medicine containing this compound. 1-2ml three times a day for a 500g adult
Prednisolone	Steroid. 0.5mg every day for acute conditions (short term) 0.25mg every other day for chronic conditions such as respiratory disease (but all steroids should be dosed at the lowest level necessary to produce a favourable response). Linked with severe side effects if continued for more than a few weeks

continued

Product	Dosage and use
Dexafort (dexamethasone)	Steroid. 0.1ml sc or im. Good following accidents such as fractures, shock and for conditions affecting the brain such as abscesses, tumours and encephalitis/meningitis
Insulin (U40 concentration)	For diabetes mellitus. Starting dose 1 unit per day before feeding. Increase by 1 unit increments until control is achieved
Millophyline	Bronchodilator. 0.4/kg every 24 hrs in acute cases. May be of help in Sendai virus pneumonia. For chronic conditions 1 dose per week combined with a steroid
Tardak (delmadinone acetate)	Anti-androgen. Dose 10mg/ml. 0.1 ml sc for a 500g rat. A second injection usually given 10 days after the first. Further injections may be required every three to four weeks. Used to treat testosterone related aggressiveness and nervousness in male animals as an alternative to castration
Fortekor (benazepril hydrochloride)	ACE inhibitor usually recommended for chronic heart failure in dogs and chronic renal insufficiency in cats. Rat owners whose vets have recommended it for the treatment of chronic heart failure in rats have found it to be very successful. Normal recommended dosage is 1mg/kg once a day. This can be increased to twice a day if symptoms indicate and if the drug is well tolerated.
Pentobarbitol	For epilepsy

2.2 Alternative remedies

2.2.1 Homoeopathic remedies

There are a lot of people who consider the practice of homoeopathy to be questionable due largely to the fact that the remedies are diluted to a point where there should be no product left. However, many clinicians consider it effective and clinical trials have shown that it can work well against certain conditions. Its uses are explained in *The Homoeopathic Treatment of Small Animals* by Christopher Day published by Daniel (ISBN 085207 216 3). A good article on homoeopathy written by vet Peter Gregory was published in *Pro-Rat-a* 93, May/June 1996, p15. A list of vets with homoeopathic qualifications is available on the British Association of Homoeopathic Veterinary Surgeons website www.bahvs.com/vetm/hom

Homoeopathic treatment is dependent on many factors, not just which disease the animal has, therefore consulting a homoeopathic vet is a good idea. However, using the 6c tablets available from chemists are good first aid. Crush them up and put them in clean drinking water, repeat daily. The dose is the same whatever the species. The following have been recommended:

Remedy	Use
Arnica	This is good for all injuries including post-operatively
Sulphur	Itchy skin conditions but must eliminate parasites first
Silicea	For chronic abscesses including pododermatitis

Homoeopathic remedies are not harmful and you could experiment with those available for treating various conditions. Others suggested are *Antinonium tartaricum* for respiratory disease, *Conium maculatum* for strokes and hindquarter paralysis in elderly bucks, *Phytolacca* for mammary tumours in does, *Arsenicum album* for diarrhoea, *Hepar sulphuris* for abscesses, Hypercal cream for chronic skin conditions such as, pododermatitis.

2.2.2 Herbal remedies

Unlike homoeopathy, there is no argument that herbal remedies can be effective. However, dosages are difficult because it is hard to know how much of an active ingredient there is in any plant. Also some can be dangerous. However, some of the herbal preparations available now are better made than they were. Remember that these compounds are still drugs and just as liable to have side effects as conventional treatments. If your rat is on any alternative medicine be sure to tell the vet, as some drugs and herbal preparations are not compatible. Unfortunately your vet may have no idea if they are or not. There is not much information on the use of herbal medicine in rats but you could try contacting the National Institute of Medical Herbalists, 54 Mary Arches Street, Exeter, Devon EX4 3BA, telephone 01392 426022, email nimh@ukexeter.freeserve.co.uk

Herbal remedies which members have recommended are:

Product	Dosage and use
Tea tree oil	Widely available from chemists. Useful for skin conditions and pododermatitis. Active against *Staphylococcus aureus* but not *Pseudomonas aeruginosa*. Preparation should contain at least 4% tea tree oil. Avoid preparations which don't give a volume.
Echinacea and golden seal	For respiratory infections. Said to lose its effectiveness if used for more than three months.
Mycoplex coriolis	A compound of a fungus used to treat or slow the growth of tumours with a good blood supply.
Ipakitine	Compound of calcium carbonate with chitin (from crustacea shells) used for absorbing phosphate from the gut. Said to help with the control of kidney failure and hind leg paralysis in elderly bucks.

continued

Product	Dosage and use
Comfrey	For pododermatis, ointment placed on the affected area and held in place with plasters. Recommended by member Rachel Rodham (*Pro-Rat-a* 105, p12) also see para 3.10.1.
Colloidal silver	Can be used on cuts and scratches
Manuka honey	For pododermatitis and ulcers, to be used topically. Needs to be placed on swabs and fixed over the affected area to prevent rats from licking it off.

2.2.3 Bach's Flower remedies

These consist of infusions prepared from freshly picked, sun exposed flowers placed in spring water and brandy. According to Bach these are meant to directly influence the patient's emotional state, thus aiding recovery. The most widely used remedy for rats is Rescue Remedy, used to treat stress. However, it is hard to say in a small animal whether the effect is due to the brandy or the flower essences. They are freely available from most pharmacies. Other ones that have been used are vine and walnut (two drops of each) for aggressive rats and a mixture of aspen, rock rose, cherry, plum and mimulus for nervous ones. In both cases the remedies were added to the drinking water for a few weeks. Recommended by member David Booker (*Pro-Rat-a* 87, p 16).

2.2.4 Other treatments

There is not the space to go over all the alternative methods of treatment. Suffice to say that if you have an interest in these then there are many to choose from! The vast majority of these are untried on rats and you should be careful when picking a practitioner, as many are untrained and have only the most rudimentary knowledge of biology, let alone medicine. This is an area where, like buying a used car, the principals of *caveat emptor* apply! If you find a treatment that works, you should write to *Pro-Rat-a* giving details.

The following book contains lots of advice on alternative treatments and is written by a vet with some 25 years' experience: *Natural Healthcare for Pets* by Richard Alport. Harper Collins. ISBN 0-00-713087-2

3 SPECIFIC DISEASES OF THE FANCY RAT

3.1 Introduction

This is not a comprehensive guide to rat diseases, there are other books mentioned in the bibliography that have further information. This section is primarily aimed at British strains of fancy rats and while most of the diseases are common to all, the incidence of diseases may change in other countries. Most of the information included is from recognised publications. Where the information has been obtained from my own or other fanciers' experiences, I have mentioned this. Each area of the body is mentioned in turn.

3.2 Head and neck

The head of the rat is the site of all the major sensory organs of the rat, including touch, which in many other mammals is principally concentrated in the front feet or hands. Apart from this the sensory organs are all well modified for the rat's life as a small opportunistic scavenger.

3.2.1 Whiskers

The whiskers or vibrissae are the major organs of touch for rats and this is one of the most important senses for them. Some dominant rats chew the whiskers off other rats in the cage, although this is more common in mice. This can be demonstrated by one rat in a cage having whiskers and all or most of the others being whiskerless. Being whiskerless disables rats by making them less sensitive to touch and they are unable to make certain size discriminations. The rats who have had their whiskers removed will regrow them. Whisker chewers should never be bred from and should be housed either alone or with a rat that is more dominant than themselves.

3.2.2 Eyes

3.2.2.1 Biology

Sight is often dismissed by some writers as a relatively unimportant sense for the rat. However, while their sight is not as good as that of a human, it is certainly important and blind rats in my experience are more nervous than their sighted colleagues. The rat eye has several adaptations and differences from the standard mammalian eye described in biology textbooks. The iris, which in most mammals reacts quickly to increased light levels by decreasing the size of the pupil, is poorly developed in the rat. This can be seen by shining a torch at a rat at night. The pupil is clearly seen and the eye may glow red for a short time. This is more pronounced in varieties with white face markings such as blazes and chinchillas who often have a condition known as heterochromia iridis (odd eye). This is usually due to aniscoria in the odd eye, where the pigment in the iris is reduced and the pupil is enlarged.

In black eyed rats the iris is pigmented, in red eyed rats there is a small amount of pigment but in pink eyed rats such as albinos there is no pigment. This pigment is there to prevent excess light getting through to the retina. In pink eyed rats the light will not be stopped. This is why they can easily suffer eye damage if exposed to excessive light levels such as sunlight or even bright artificial light. The rat has a much larger lens in proportion to a human lens, due to it being chiefly a nocturnal animal; the larger lens is used to make use of lower light levels. Because of this, rats have good light sensitivity. Due to the size of the lens and the relatively small size of the eye, its shape cannot be altered much, meaning that rats are short sighted.

The position of the rat's eyes, on the sides of the head, means that they have a wide area of view, so that they can see very well to the side as well as in front. They also have a good overlap of stereoscopic vision to the front which means that they can judge distances well for jumping etc. It is a myth that rats hold their heads on one side to look at you. Pink eyed rats appear to have some problem with this and will weave from side to side to improve their perspective.

The retina in dark eyed rats has an outer pigmented layer that prevents internal reflections in the eye but this is absent in pink eyed rats. The inner layer is made up of the light sensitive rods and cones. Rods respond to lower light levels than cones but the image is seen in black and white, which is why you do not see in colour at night. Cones are responsible for colour vision. There are several different types of cones depending on what region of the colour spectrum they respond to. There are cones which respond to red, green, blue and ultraviolet light. There is some argument in textbooks regarding rats, from those who say that rats have no cones and therefore can only see in black and white, to those who say that they do have cones and can detect some colours, but are effectively red/green colour blind, like most mammals except primates. However, as rats certainly do have cones (although fewer than we do) I would suggest that 'the rat can only see in black and white' hypothesis is past its sell by date. The reason most mammals are red/green colour blind is because they only have two of the three types of cones (blue and green detectors) that you need for complete colour vision. I have even heard on a radio broadcast that rats (and some other mammals) have cones which can detect ultraviolet light, a facility normally reported for animals other than mammals such as birds and insects.

The messages from the retina are sent to the brain via a network of nerve fibres. However, once more the poor albino loses out, because in their case much of this network is incorrectly wired. The actual effect of this is unclear although work with albino mice shows that they make more mistakes in black/white discrimination tests.

3.2.2.2 Signs of ill health

Eyes should be bright and bold with no discharge or clouding. Some rats normally have more sunken eyes than others. It is important that you know your own animal. Symptoms of problems include swelling, reddish discharge and crusting around the eyes, sunken eyes, clouding or opacity of one or both eyes.

3.2.2.2.1 Red stained discharge and crusting around both eyes

The red stained discharge from the eyes and nose of the rat are stained with porphyrins, not blood. Normally only small amounts are produced. They are produced by the Harderian glands which are situated around the eye socket. Under stresses such as showing, heat or illness the amount of discharge can increase.

The commonest cause of the severe symptoms mentioned above are a viral infection called rat coronavirus (RCV). There are two types of virus which cause this problem. They are sialodacryoadenitis virus (SDAV) and Parker's coronavirus (PCV). This starts suddenly and normally lasts 10 to 14 days. Sometimes rats with this will also exhibit snuffling, other respiratory symptoms and swelling of the neck and face. Most rats make a complete recovery but some will develop a long term keratoconjunctivitis which will make the eye appear clouded. This is because of drying of the eyes due to decreased tears. Secondary infections with the bacterium *Staphylococcus aureus* occasionally occur. Eye discomfort will sometimes cause a rat to scratch at its eyes causing serious damage including the loss of an eye. SDAV is commoner in the UK in late summer/early autumn but sometimes outbreaks occur in the spring. Rats usually get the condition once only as it confers long lasting immunity. The most serious infections are suffered by two to four week old rats whose mothers have never had the infection and therefore have no protective antibody. It is contracted by being in the vicinity of an infected rat as it is an airborne virus. Rats secrete the virus for seven days. It is extremely contagious. Direct contact is not necessary. No treatment is available for the virus but the eyes can be bathed in warm saline if you like. When secondary infection occurs antibiotic cream or drops can be used. It is wise not to show or sell rats while you have an outbreak. This virus is not carried by healthy rats and when the outbreak ends your stock is clear until it comes in contact with it again. Some severe outbreaks among fancy and pet rats leading to fatalities have been reported from the US.

If the discharge occurs in one eye only or if it lasts longer than a few days there may be a bacterial infection or foreign body present. Veterinary advice should be sought. Antibiotic drops containing chloramphenicol can be used to treat bacterial eye infections. If the condition persists in spite of treatment, it is advisable not to breed with this rat as it may have an ingrowing eyelash or other potentially hereditary condition.

3.2.2.2.2 Injury

Deb Mallett

Eye damage in left eye

This is usually caused by a scratch or a debris particle and is a complication of rat coronavirus infection due to the irritation caused. The eye usually swells alarmingly and scabs over. The eyeball is often destroyed but it will heal in time. A vet may advise the removal of the eyeball but this is not usually necessary. Bathing and antibiotic cream may help. There are not normally any long term problems except blindness on that side.

3.2.2.2.3 Cataracts

Rats with cataracts have a milky white centre to the eye caused by clouding of the lens and causes at least partial blindness in the affected eye. It may affect one or both sides. Cataracts are often hereditary and affected rats should not be bred from. Most of the recognised genetic cataracts in laboratories have been reported in very young rats. However, I have seen it develop in older rats as well. It can affect pink or black eyed rats. There is no treatment in rats. It may also follow infection.

3.2.2.2.4 Blindness

Sight is not the most important sense in the rat and they can manage without it. One sided blindness probably will not affect them at all. Completely blind rats will use their other senses more to compensate but should not be allowed to jump although most will not attempt to. They are quite clever and do not usually fall, however, playtimes should be supervised just in case. It is not necessary to remove platforms etc from cages as they will quickly learn the confines of their cage. Do not change their environment too radically if you can avoid it. Some blind rats can be quite nervous and require a quiet home.

3.2.2.2.5 Eye deformities

Kittens are sometimes born with eye deformities. These show themselves when their eyes first open. There are several types and some are genetic. One that seems to occur occasionally in fancy stock in the UK gives eyes that are smaller than normal and appear transparent, so that the blood vessels in the eye are clearly visible. It is not known whether this is caused by a virus attacking the embryo or a genetic effect. When it occurs it will affect at least half the litter and it can be on one or both sides. It is usually reported in pink eyed rats, but this may just be because it does not show up in dark eyed rats.

Occasionally a rat may be born with one eye smaller than the other, or even lacking an eye completely. These rats should not be bred from, and the stock they are bred from should be considered suspect. This appears to be a threshold trait and as such can often occur when two unrelated strains are crossed. There is also a marked maternal influence on the inheritance. This may be due either to arrested development in the uterus or possibly because it is a trait more likely to be passed on by the doe.

A condition known as 'fatty eye' has been reported in Sweden amongst black eyed white rats of UK extraction. This condition affects the tissues immediately surrounding the eye and appears to be a small benign tumour of the tear or Harderian glands. Steps have been taken in Sweden to prevent breeding from affected lines. This condition has not been reported in the UK.

3.2.2.2.6 Sunken eyes

These can be a sign of dehydration or pain. Other dehydration symptoms include thin appearance of the extremities, and a pinched up area of skin remains peaked for some time instead of immediately springing back. Other pain symptoms may include tooth chattering, sitting hunched or tucked up, staring coat and a marked lack of interest in their surroundings.

3.2.2.2.7 Photophobia

This is a dislike of light more intense than normal for that animal. It may show itself by increased blinking or by the rat actively trying to avoid the light. It is sometimes seen in pink eyed whites who have had too much exposure to the sun. A day or two kept quiet in a room away from direct sunlight will solve the problem. This symptom is also an early sign of SDAV or occasionally something more sinister such as encephalitis.

3.2.2.2.8 Eye bulging

This is normally seen when a contented rat is tooth grinding (bruxing). It is not a problem, probably just a habit like thumb sucking in humans.

3.2.2.2.9 Swelling of the eye and surrounding tissues

If seen in pink eyed whites on a sunny day and affecting both eyes this is probably due to overexposure to sunlight. On other occasions however this could be the beginning of SDAV. If only one eye is affected there could be a serious infection behind the eye that requires treatment. If the swelling appears over a few weeks, it could be due to a tumour behind the eye.

3.2.3 Ears

The hearing of the rat is relatively good and is at its best at higher frequency sounds. This is because rats communicate vocally by means of high pitched noises which we are unable to hear. Vocal communication is important in rat communities and deaf rats are at a social disadvantage. Black eyed white rats, like blue eyed white cats are often deaf due to abnormalities in the organ of Corti in the inner ear. This is the site where sound vibrations are detected. Hearing happens by sound vibrations disturbing hairs in the organ of Corti and this message being transferred via nerves to the brain. These hairs are modifications of normal body hairs and in those rats with no melanocytes these hair cells seem unable to function. Pink eyed rats, which do have melanocytes, are not deaf.

Rat ears are normally erect, clean, with no discharge. Wax is not normally visible. Rats do not normally scratch their ears much. Problems may be indicated by ears carried flat, discharge, scabs and warty patches around the edge of the ear.

3.2.3.1 Ears carried flat to the skull

This can be a sign of pain, dehydration, hypothermia and/or stress but some rats will do this at rest.

3.2.3.2 Shaking and vibration of ears and neck

This is a normal sign of oestrus (heat) in female rats and indicates readiness to mate.

3.2.3.3 Red ears

This is caused by increased blood flow through the ears. The rats are trying to lose heat through the ears and it is commonly seen in bucks at shows, or sometimes in rats after surgery. It is an early sign of heat stress.

3.2.3.4 Dry scabs and warty growths around the edge of the ears (ear mange)

Rat with ear mange mites

When these occur they are normally seen on the tail as well. They can also be seen on the genitalia, nose and anywhere else where the fur is thin and the skin comparatively cool. They indicate infection with the mange mite *Notoedres muris*. This was a common problem in the Edwardian fancy but is rare now. It is more common in situations of overcrowding and poor husbandry and thus is sometimes brought in via rescue or pet shop rats. It can be treated with ivermectin. The edge of the ears may be permanently damaged. The Edwardians used to treat this with a mix of Jeyes fluid, flowers of sulphur and Vaseline that appeared to work well although I would not recommend this now. This condition is caught directly off another rat and not off hay and so on. The presence of dichlorvos fly killer strips in the rattery will also prevent this condition.

The same rat – now successfully treated

3.2.3.5 Hair dryers

Ears can be damaged by hair dryers set on too high a setting. This can burn and dry the edges of the ears out. They will then crack off. Wet rats should be towel dried and hair dryers only used on the coolest setting.

3.2.3.6 Ear discharge

An ear discharge is normally due to a middle ear infection or a foreign body lodged in the ear. Affected rats may shake their head or scratch their ears excessively. The discharge is caused by pus which has built up behind the ear drum bursting it. If an infection spreads to the inner ear the rat may carry its head to one side (see next paragraph). After the ear drum has burst the infection will usually clear up although it may recur. A course of an antibiotic selected to have good penetration into the ear, such as chloramphenicol (if available) or azithromycin may help prevent the rare complications. The infection is usually caused by respiratory organisms, typically *Mycoplasma, Pasteurella pneumotropica* and *Streptococcus pneumoniae*.

3.2.3.7 Middle/inner ear disease, torticollis, wry neck, head tilt, labyrinthitis

This common condition shows itself by the rat holding its head to one side. If you hold the rat up by its tail it will spin around. It occurs suddenly and may follow an attack of snuffles. It has many names. Labyrinthitis is probably the most correct when the condition is due, as it normally is, to an infection of the inner ear. It is not life threatening and generally occurs in adolescents and young adults.

The symptoms are caused by an infection of the inner ear, including the semi-circular canals which govern balance. The infection has usually got into the inner ear via the middle ear and the Eustachian tube, although this does not mean that the organisms have caused disease in the middle ear. The organisms that cause the infection are usually respiratory and include *Mycoplasma pulmonis* and *Streptococcus pneumoniae*. Treatment with antibiotics may help if started early enough but even without treatment most rats make a partial recovery within a month. If you are going to treat it you need to use an antibiotic (chloramphenicol if available, otherwise azithromycin) that can penetrate the inner ear. Even with treatment, however, most rats that have had this condition can be spotted by the experienced observer.

Fanciers should not breed with affected rats because it is possible that a predisposition to develop this is hereditary. Rats with this condition cannot be shown.

Rats sometimes suffer head tilt due to other causes, including pituitary tumours, meningitis and strokes. These are all rarer and more serious conditions that are covered under separate headings in this section. Pituitary tumours and strokes tend to occur in older rats.

3.2.4 Teeth and mouth

Rats have 16 teeth. Four incisors, which are bright orange in the healthy rat and are visible, and 12 molars which are at the back of the jaw and very difficult to see without a general anaesthetic. Rats have no canines or premolars. The incisors are open rooted and therefore grow throughout the rat's life. While it is a myth that rats must gnaw hard foods in order to keep their teeth down it is necessary that the opposing incisors meet. Unlike rabbits and some other rodents, whose molars are also open rooted; the molars of rats grow very slowly but only when there is the pressure of another tooth. Therefore there is no risk of the molars overgrowing unless the teeth are seriously misaligned, meaning that it is theoretically possible that spurs of tooth enamel could form. Rats, like other rodents have only one set of teeth in their lifetime. There are mutations that lack incisors entirely. These rats should not be bred from.

3.2.4.1 Malocclusion

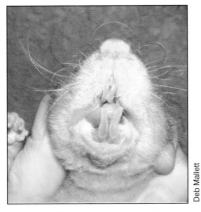

Rat with maloccluded teeth

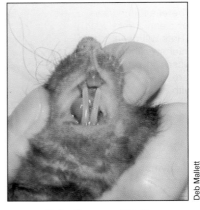

Rat with normal teeth

Young rats - This is usually noticed at weaning or just after. The rat starts to lose weight and its top lip appears swollen and misshapen. When the teeth are examined, one or both bottom incisors will be misaligned with the top set. This will cause uncontrolled tooth growth. Without treatment the rat will suffer much pain and probably eventually die as the teeth can penetrate the cheek, jaw, face or brain. The overgrown parts of the teeth must be clipped regularly every 10 days. You can do this yourself (perhaps with help) with nail clippers or small wire cutters. It is not painful (the incisors have no nerves) but the rats are not keen. It is important that you do not twist the tooth while you are clipping as you may damage the tooth or jaw. You should also wear eye protection as otherwise a flying shard of extremely sharp tooth could hit you or your helper in the eye! It is not desirable or practical to anaesthetise a rat every 10 days, although sedation with diazepam can be used. It is possible to completely remove these teeth by surgery. More information about this is given in *The Handbook of Rabbit and Rodent Medicine* listed in the bibliography. However, for some reason, judging from the feedback I have received, this operation appears to carry a high failure and mortality rate. If you decide to have it done, you should ask the vet about their experience with this operation in *rats*. An alternative treatment that has been tried was drilling out the affected teeth and then the roots were killed with formalcresol. Affected rats should not be bred from.

Older rats - Older rats may develop malocclusion due to a broken tooth or damage to the jaw. The treatment is the same except that when the broken tooth has regrown, clipping may no longer be necessary. For clipping the teeth of an adult it is advisable to wrap the rat in a towel first unless they are very placid.

3.2.4.2 Discoloration of the teeth

The upper incisors of the rat are usually bright orange, the bottom ones paler. Any other colour may indicate a problem. Special problems include horizontal lines in the teeth causing weakness and fractures, thin enamel, deformed teeth. Causes include too much or too little vitamin A and D, treatment with tetracyclines in young rats and excess fluoride. The cause should be investigated and is comprehensively dealt with in *The Rat in Laboratory Investigation* edited by Ferris and Griffiths. This book is out of print but can be obtained through the British Library.

3.2.4.3 Tooth decay

Whereas the incisors do not suffer from tooth decay the molars certainly do! As you cannot clean a rat's teeth it is important not to feed sweet things as more than a rare treat. Rats will develop abscesses on the roots of decayed teeth. These will show up as a painful swelling of the jaw. Antibiotics should help to clear up the infection but tooth abscesses in rats must be considered serious and require veterinary advice. Luckily, they are virtually unknown in rats fed a proper diet, although it is possible to select for rats with a high incidence of molar tooth decay.

3.2.4.4 Swellings on or under the jaw

This can be due to a tooth abscess, bone tumours, infected lymph nodes, rat coronavirus or lymphoma (cancer of the lymph nodes, especially histiocytic sarcoma). Infected lymph nodes should clear up within a few days and antibiotics should help if necessary. If the lymph node continues to enlarge and others, especially in the neck and armpits, emerge it is possible that the rat has lymphoma. It is possible that in rare cases this is caused by a virus and is transmissible. It is said that cancer causing viruses, while they do exist for rats, do not appear to cause disease (although they certainly do for mice and hamsters!). However, many years ago, for a period of about five years I had a problem with lymphoma cropping up in over 50% of my rats. The only thing that these rats had in common was that all, at some time, had shared a cage. The disease stopped spreading when all affected animals and their contacts were separated from my other animals. If these symptoms occur in your rats, especially if they are under one year old, it is better to treat it as an infectious disease spread by direct contact.

Occasionally whole grains or the husk may penetrate the mouth tissue, causing abscesses and swellings in the mouth. These will probably require treatment to remove the offending material. These injuries are rare however and should not put you off using whole grains, which are a valuable food.

3.2.5 Swaying

Some rats, usually pink eyed ones, will sway from side to side. This is more noticeable around the head and neck. This is quite normal and is a technique used by the rat to help them to judge distance. Pink eyed rats have inferior vision to rats with dark eyes.

3.3 Respiratory tract

This is made up of the upper respiratory tract – nose, sinuses, pharynx, throat and bronchus –– and the lower respiratory tract – bronchioles and alveoli. The upper respiratory tract contains a mixed bacterial flora while the lower respiratory tract is relatively sterile. Bacteria are removed by being trapped in the mucus produced by the lungs. This mucus is then wafted out by minute hairs (cilia) found on the surface of the passageways in the lungs. The lungs also have their own white blood cells to fight infection.

3.3.1 Coughing and choking

Rats do not cough as such but they can sneeze out particles and mucus. They also have a choking reflex to remove food objects that become stuck. This reflex is quite violent and distressing for the rat, let alone any concerned onlookers! However, it is quite normal and is the only way a rat has to clear such objects. Rats are best left to recover by themselves. However, if the rat has difficulty breathing or the fingertips start to turn blue then pick up the rat, hold it head downwards with his back across your palm and tail along your arm. Hold on to the base of the tail with your other hand. Swing the rat downward sharply several times, remembering to support the head and neck to prevent accidental dislocation. Check the rat to see if this has dislodged the debris. Veterinary advice is helpful only if the rat can be seen within a very short time.

3.3.2 Nose bleeds

The appearance of a slight amount of red discharge around the nose is not unusual and is more likely to be due to porphyrins than blood. These pigments are made in the Harderian gland. Where the discharge is sticky and remains around the nose this is likely to be due to infection with *Streptococcus pneumoniae* or sialodacryoadenitis virus (SDAV) (see next paragraph 3.3.3). Occasionally rats will haemorrhage quite badly from the nose. Usually there will have been some symptoms before this, either a slight amount of blood from the nose or some respiratory symptoms. The reasons for heavy nose bleeds may be due to many causes, including chronic infection of the upper respiratory tract, nasal polyps, clotting defects and very rarely tumours. The reasons should be investigated.

3.3.3 Symptoms of respiratory disease

Rats are very susceptible to respiratory problems both of the upper and lower respiratory tract. It is important to differentiate between the two. Upper respiratory tract infections are usually trivial and include rhinitis (cold symptoms), sinusitis and sometimes ear and eye infections as well. Lower respiratory tract infections may follow on from upper respiratory infections and include bronchitis and pneumonia. These can lead to chronic bronchitis and emphysema. All respiratory disease tends to be called 'snuffles' by fanciers because of the rattling or whiffling noise the rat makes when breathing. Sometimes, if you hold a rat you can feel the vibrations of their rough breathing through the chest wall. However, you should not conclude from this that the infection is always in the chest. Most of the time if the rat is looking otherwise fit the infection is in the sinuses, it just sounds and feels as if it is in the chest because the chest acts like an amplifier to breathing sounds.

Pneumonia is an acute disease that requires immediate treatment. The rat normally lies in its bed, will not eat or sometimes drink either, has a staring coat and eyes and difficulty breathing (dyspnoea). Sometimes it is more of a gasp. If this happens the prognosis is very bad. Treatment includes regular turning, giving fluids, antibiotics, products to keep the airways open, sometimes steroids such as prednisolone, and keeping the rat warm but well ventilated.

Chronic bronchitis and emphysema are normally present in rats with long term respiratory disease. It is not possible to cure it as there are permanent pathological changes in the lungs as well as chronic infections. Antibiotics may control the disease but will not kill all the bacteria and cannot mend the damage. In emphysema the lungs have lost much of their elasticity and breathing becomes difficult. Decongestants and drugs which keep the airways open may help.

3.3.3.1 Causes

Most respiratory disease in rats is caused by the bacteria that the rats carry normally. A decrease in immunity due to stress, damp, operations, age, pregnancy and so on may then lead to an increase in the numbers or pathogenicity of these organisms. Organisms that rats carry that can cause infections include *Mycoplasma pulmonis, Streptobacillus moniliformis, Corynebacterium kutscheri, Pasteurella pneumotropica, Streptococcus pneumoniae, Streptococcus zooepidemicus*, cilia associated respiratory bacillus (CAR bacillus) and occasionally *Salmonella* species. In addition to these there are organisms that rats generally have to catch from another rat, other animal or the environment. These include the viruses; SDAV, Parker's rat coronavirus and Sendai virus, the bacteria *Bordetella bronchiseptica* and *Haemophilus* and the fungus *Aspergillus*. Bladder worms (*Trichosomoides crassicauda*) can cause a short lived parasitic bronchitis when the parasite is undergoing the migratory stage of its life cycle.

It is not normally possible to tell one infection from another without tests although *Mycoplasma pulmonis, Streptococcus pneumoniae* and *Corynebacterium kutscheri* are the most common bacterial infections. Sendai and SDAV are the most common viral infections. All except mycoplasmosis and *Pasteurella* infection, which develops slowly, tend to have rapid onset.

Mycoplasma pulmonis is the most important respiratory pathogen in the UK in rats over three months old due to its ubiquitous nature. It is likely that all of the pet and fancy rats in the UK are carrying this organism. The disease is without symptoms in the beginning and by the time the rat is showing symptoms the infection is usually well established. Initial symptoms include rhinitis and textbooks say that the disease is chronic and progressive, leading to worsening chest infection and pneumonia after several months. Many breeders however find that their rats either do not show any symptoms or may have minor respiratory symptoms for a few weeks. Sometimes infection progresses to a more chronic condition involving the sinuses but rarely to anything more serious. In pet shop and rescue rats more serious symptoms, including pneumonia, frequently develop. This lack of symptoms in fancy rats could be due to the fancier selecting against rats that show symptoms and/or good husbandry. It is known that susceptibility to this condition is under genetic control. The disease is caused initially by the organism attaching itself to the cell membrane in the respiratory tract, probably very early in life. Then the organism multiplies itself and produces a mitogen (a chemical that induces cell growth) that in susceptible rats causes an overgrowth of immune tissue called bronchus associated lymphatic tissue (BALT). *Mycoplasma* can also resist being eaten by the white cells (in particular alveolar macrophages) in these susceptible rats. In unsusceptible rats macrophages remain active and the overgrowth of tissue is not so pronounced. Infected rats do produce antibodies but these do not appear to protect against the infection. However, they do appear to prevent the spread of infection to other sites such as the genital tract.

In susceptible rats, tissue growth will continue and impair lung function. This damage is not reversible. However, unless there is a concurrent infection with another bacterial pathogen, *Mycoplasma* does not normally form lung abscesses. Antibiotic treatment is rarely permanently successful against this disease as no antibiotic will remove all the organisms. They rely on the patient being able to control the remainder. In *Mycoplasma* susceptible rats however, the animal is quite unable to do this so that the infection just comes back. The disease is made worse by high ammonia and carbon dioxide levels and simultaneous infection with Sendai or rat coronaviruses, CAR bacillus, *Streptococcus pneumoniae, Pasteurella pneumotropica* and *Corynebacterium kutscheri*. Infact some researchers consider that for *Mycoplasma* to become established there has to be simultaneous infection with a respiratory virus and high ammonia levels.

Streptococcus pneumoniae is carried in the upper respiratory tract of many mammals and generally does not cause disease. Disease may occur following travel (such as going to shows), during the winter months and in rats on minimal diets. It may occur as a secondary infection to other respiratory infections. The first stage of illness is generally a slightly bloodstained (not caused by porphyrins this time), thickish nasal discharge that sticks to the fur around the nose. Sometimes the inside of the fore paw may become stained with the discharge as the rat attempts to wipe it away. This can progress to rhinitis, sinusitis, conjunctivitis and otitis media (middle ear infection - see ear discharge 3.2.3.6). It can then go on to cause acute chest infection with weight loss, lack of appetite, dyspnoea and occasional head tilt. It can progress rapidly to pneumonia and death. Unlike *Mycoplasma*, this infection comes on rapidly. It is treatable with the correct antibiotics although resistance can be a problem. Erythromycin and penicillin can be used. Benzylpenicillin dosed at a rate of 150 units/g body weight has been used successfully. Enrofloxacin (Baytril) is not the drug of first choice against this organism. *Streptococcus pneumoniae* may be passed on from humans to rats. However, this organism is not the same as the *Streptococcus* responsible for 'Strep throats' in humans. That species is *Streptococcus pyogenes*, which does not cause respiratory infections in rats.

Corynebacterium kutscheri is a normal inhabitant of the mouth. It is an opportunist pathogen and things that predispose to it causing infection are; nutritional deficiencies, steroid treatment, pregnancy, inadequate hygiene and *Salmonella* infection. Other respiratory infections do not appear to start it off. It is an acute disease that makes the

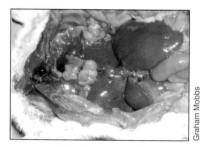 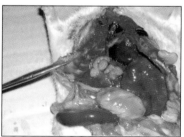

Nodules in a rat's lung caused by Corynebacterium kutscheri

rats very ill but the mortality rate is only around 10%. If it is going to kill the rat it usually dies within the week. The symptoms are: staring coat, emaciation, rapid respiration, hunched position, abnormal gait, nasal and ocular discharge, lethargy and sometimes septic and swollen joints. Unlike other respiratory infections it does not seem to produce snuffling. Severe infection may lead to loss of toes. During the course of the infection the organism is widespread throughout the rat's body, sometimes causing abscesses. This is often seen in rats on long term steroid therapy. Abscesses often appear on the lungs which is why this disease is sometimes called pseudotuberculosis. These lung abscesses are full of a substance that resembles cream cheese. In survivors the abscesses usually become walled off and inactive after the infection is over. The organism can be treated using ampicillin, chloramphenicol and tetracycline; however, this frequently just suppresses the infection, which will come back as soon as treatment is stopped. Therefore it is probably better to let it run its course.

Bordetella bronchiseptica rarely causes disease in rats but at least three outbreaks in the fancy have been recorded. In the first case the rats caught the organism from the owner's dogs which had kennel cough at this time due to *B. bronchiseptica*. The infection, which was confirmed by culture, caused a rapidly fatal pneumonia (sometimes within a few hours), suggesting that the rats had no natural defences against this organism. If you have dogs, it is wise to isolate them from your rats if you suspect kennel cough. In a second case it is not sure where the infection came from. In all cases about a third of the rats died. They were all middle aged or older. Good hygiene technique to stop your clothes, hair and so on contaminating your rats should also be observed. In this case, treatment was unsuccessful. However, this organism can theoretically be treated using erythromycin, chloramphenicol, trimethoprim sulpha drugs, such as Tribrissen, Septrin or Baytril. Kennel cough vaccine is a live vaccine inoculated into the dog's nose. This is possibly infectious for rats for a week or so. So keep newly vaccinated dogs away.

Pasteurella pneumotropica is normally carried in the upper respiratory tract, uterus and gastrointestinal tract. Rats are believed to become infected at weaning via the nasopharynx, presumably as they are losing maternal antibody. In most rats this organism probably does not cause disease but it can be responsible for causing respiratory disease including bronchopneumonia, conjunctivitis, abscesses, abortion, mastitis, infertility and middle ear infection. It will complicate *Mycoplasma* infection. Treatment is with chloramphenicol, ampicillin, enrofloxacin or cephalexin. It is difficult to differentiate it from *Mycoplasma* from the clinical symptoms.

Cilia associated respiratory bacillus (CAR) is an unclassified organism sometimes associated with respiratory disease in rats. It is found in the respiratory tracts of many animals but its role in disease is uncertain. There is no convincing evidence that it can cause a natural disease outbreak by itself but it can act as a co-pathogen alongside *Mycoplasma* or Sendai virus. The organism embeds itself among the cilia, interfering with their action. The tissues may become thickened and produce more mucus. Transmission is by direct contact. Although various antibiotics have been used to treat possible infections, it is not certain how successful any of these were.

There are at least three viruses that can cause respiratory disease. These are Parker's rat coronavirus, SDAV (another coronavirus) (both of these also cause eye disease 3.2.2.2.1) and Sendai virus. Sendai virus frequently attacks kittens, leading to short lived cold symptoms (rhinitis). Kittens are protected by maternal antibody until they are four to six weeks old, when they become susceptible to infection. The infections are usually minor and lead to immunity. However, in kittens with no maternal antibody because the mother has never had the infection, the disease can strike younger and be much more severe. Occasionally adults with no previous contact may get an attack which presents as a staring coat with shortness of breath. Severely affected rats may gasp for breath and these frequently die. The bronchodilator Millophyline may help these rats. Rhinitis is rare in adults. A bad attack can cause does to produce dead litters. This is not because the kittens have been infected but because the doe is not able to obtain enough oxygen to supply both her and the foetuses.

Most viral infections are short lived but can allow previously mentioned bacteria present to multiply and cause a more serious secondary infection. These viruses are probably very common in the showing population. The outbreak in an establishment lasts as long as it takes to infect all the rats. There appears to be no carrier state.

Generally, if an infection is limited to the upper respiratory tract it will usually clear up after a couple of weeks unless there is sinus involvement. Infections of the lower respiratory tract and sinuses are cleared with difficulty and most rats will then snuffle a bit all of their lives, mostly due to scar tissue and the continuing presence of *Mycoplasma*.

3.3.3.2 Control and treatment

Respiratory conditions are made worse when poor husbandry allows ammonia and carbon dioxide gases to build up. This can be controlled by regular cleaning, good ventilation and/or not overstocking. Some people have suggested that some types of sawdust and shavings can cause snuffles or make them worse, due to the presence of phenols in the resin. The scientific evidence for this in rats is poor however and British laboratories routinely use softwood shavings. Most of the negative information concerns products made from cedar and pine but the principal species used in the UK is the Sitka spruce (source: the Forestry Commission), which does not appear to have the same implications. However, high dust levels in some bedding may cause problems and fine sawdust and clay cat litters should be avoided. Try to use dust extracted wood shavings. Mouldy or dusty hay can also be a problem, therefore use good quality hay only or otherwise use shredded paper.

New rats when first introduced to a stud may become ill due to contact with the other rats' microbes, or *vice versa*, alternatively this may happen at a show. It is not unknown for new fanciers to take home pathogens from shows and have their stock nearly wiped out while the rat that gave it to them at the show may be showing no symptoms at all. This does not usually happen to more regular fanciers, presumably because their stock is immune or not susceptible. It is therefore advisable to quarantine show stock for a few days after returning. With respiratory infections it is difficult to prevent infection but screens between cages can help, although it is better to keep infected rats in a separate place. Some owners use Olbas oil and other strong smelling plant oils to ease breathing, and the use of soluble aspirin, pseudoephedrine and Millophyline (doses given in the drugs list section 2.1.6) can also help. These treatments do not cure the rat but can ease the symptoms.

Successful antibiotic treatment varies with the organism. Treating minor symptoms is unnecessary, the rat's own immune system should be given the chance to clear the infection, and if a rat is not obviously ill then it is probably better not to use antibiotics. As has been explained, *Mycoplasma* infection is probably incurable although it can be controlled in snuffling rats using azithromycin, tetracyclines and enrofloxacin (Baytril). A complete cure is probably not possible due to the chronic tissue damage that has occurred and the rat's inability to clear the organism. (Also many rats who snuffle but appear otherwise healthy have chronic sinusitis. This is difficult for most antibiotics including enrofloxacin to penetrate properly. The tetracycline, doxycycline can penetrate the sinuses and is also active against *Mycoplasma*.) The symptoms may be controlled in the short term but either it or another organism will just come back when the treatment is finished. Also during prolonged treatment the organism may become resistant to the antibiotic. If you are going to use long term treatment then it is better to alternate between two or three different antibiotics.

Some other bacterial respiratory diseases appear more treatable. Treatment to alleviate the symptoms using steroids such as prednisolone can be used under veterinary advice although this may increase the likelihood of infection with *Corynebacterium kutscheri* if the treatment is prolonged. Homoeopathic remedies may help but for best effect it is advisable to consult a homoeopathic vet. *Antinonium tartaricum* has been recommended.

As has already been mentioned, most fanciers cull chronic snufflers or at least do not breed from them and respiratory disease has become mild in most studs. This indicates that selection for those resistant to the disease is successful, although it could also be due to those studs looking after their rats differently. There is no evidence that chronic snufflers are infectious to other rats.

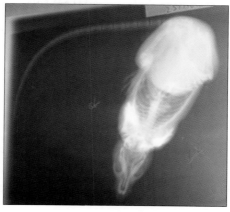

*X-ray of rat which later died of
chronic lung disease*

Respiratory symptoms can be caused by other physiological factors including kidney and heart failure. This usually occurs in old rats and is incurable (see kidney 3.5.3 and heart disease 3.4). Some rats will develop difficulty breathing when treated with anti-mite sprays. If this occurs the rat usually recovers after a few hours. Veterinary treatment may be helpful.

3.3.3.3 Asthma

Traditionally all snuffles in rats was referred to as 'asthma'. Then the term went out of fashion among fanciers. However the Brown Norway rat has been used as an animal model for asthma research and they certainly can get it. Affected rats become allergic to specific inhaled substances in their environment. The respiratory symptoms produced come on rapidly and can be severe but they usually subside in a few hours unlike respiratory disease caused by an infectious agent. The symptoms include everything from a mild wheeze to the rat gasping for breath. A vet can prescribe something such as Millophyline or an antihistamine which may help attacks. However it is better to try to isolate the allergen and keep it away from the rat. Some anti-mite sprays have been shown to cause this in some rats. Asthmatic rats should not be bred from as the tendency is inherited.

3.4 Heart

Symptomatic heart disease is rare in rats although if the heart is examined, degenerative changes can be observed in rats over one year. Signs may include difficulty breathing, blue tips to the toes and tail and fluid retention. These can also occur with chronic lung disease. The two commonest forms of heart disease are dilated cardiomyopathy, where the heart becomes enlarged and flabby, and hypertrophic cardiomyopathy, where the heart becomes thickened and stiff due to overwork. The former leads to a build up of fluid under the skin and the latter a build up of fluid in the lungs. It is important that the correct diagnosis is made as the treatments, if used, vary. Recommended treatments (Debbie Ducommun's) are, a low sodium diet, a diuretic such as Lasix (frusemide) dose 2-4mg/kg one to three times a day, and an ACE inhibitor such as enalapril dose 0.05mg/kg once daily. For dilated cardiomyopathy a digitalis derivative may be recommended although this carries more risk. Cardoxin, dose 0.002-0.005 mg/kg BID has been used. Alternative dietary supplements including omega-3 fatty acids found in fish oils and flax oil (25mg/day), Co-enzyme Q10 30mg/day, L-carnitine 25mg/day and taurine 50mg/day have been used successfully by some. However, it should be remembered that all these treatments are not cures but are there to relieve symptoms.

To avoid problems you should control your rat's weight and feed a good balanced diet to all stock. The seeds of heart disease are sown in the nest so it is important that young rats receive the correct diet. A couple of recent cases of young rats dying suddenly showed no symptoms except enlarged hearts. These kittens were also classed as obese and hence it is imperative that young rats are not allowed to get too fat.

3.4.1 Infectious heart disease

A condition which appears to be transmissible causes enlarged atria and sudden death in infected rats. All ages may be affected. There are no symptoms. It has been postulated that this may be Coxsackie B virus. However there are no reports in the literature.

3.5 Urinary system

This includes the kidneys, ureters, bladder and urethra. Urine is normally clear and yellowish. In males it is strong smelling, sticky and in addition when they are marking their territory they tend to leave trails of it around. This is quite normal although rather annoying. It is easily sponged off. Rat urine is sticky because it includes a molecule called lipocaliene. This molecule contains the rat's smell message and is designed to slowly release this scent. These molecules are being developed for a number of commercial applications.

People who are allergic to rats are normally affected by the proteins in the urine, not the fur.

3.5.1 Cystitis/pyelonephritis

In rats acute cystitis/pyelonephritis is often not noticed until a rat starts to produce blood stained urine. The rat may sit hunched up with hollowed flanks and a staring coat if it is in pain. Weight loss and even death may follow. The urine can be investigated better by placing the rat in a clean plastic tank without bedding and waiting for it to urinate. Blood stained and cloudy urine can be indicative of cystitis. It is usually caused by a bacterial infection of the bladder (cystitis) or kidneys (pyelonephritis). *Streptococcus pneumoniae* is reported to produce blood stained urine (haematuria) but probably many other bacteria can do it as well. These diseases are very treatable providing the right antibiotic in the right concentration is used. It may be necessary to have an antibiotic sensitivity test done on the causative organism. It is important that the rat drinks plenty of water.

3.5.2 Bladder crystals/stones

This condition presents with similar symptoms to cystitis but if the urine is examined under a low power microscope, crystals will be seen. These crystals have sharp edges which cause pain and bleeding. The condition can be caused by a bacterial infection, the presence of bladder worms or possibly diet. In rabbits unbalanced high calcium diets have been linked with this but it is unclear whether this is also true for rats. The type of crystal present is influenced by diet and the pH of the urine. Treatment is by diet and treatment of the underlying cause. Only fresh urine samples should be examined as crystals may form in stored samples, especially when these are stored in the fridge.

3.5.3 Chronic kidney disease

Many rats (especially bucks) over 18 months old may have kidney damage without showing any symptoms. They will have protein in their urine although you have to be a bit careful of this as some protein in the urine is normal in the rat. It is important that the test used detects albumin or other serum proteins and not just any protein. Health problems are usually only seen in rats over two years old. The two conditions which may both be present are chronic pyelonephritis and focal segment glomerulosclerosis (FSGS) which tends to follow the other.

Affected rats may show progressive weight loss especially over the back and loin, loss of condition and increasing weakness although old rats show these signs for other reasons. This condition is also linked to hind leg paralysis. When the condition becomes terminal the rat appears to develop respiratory disease due to fluid build up in the lungs. Kidney disease is not the inevitable outcome of old age and may be linked either to high protein or high calorie diets fed ad lib throughout life. Diets low in potassium or high in phosphate also seem to be linked to this condition. Rats homozygous for the red eye yellow gene *r*, that is the UK varieties topaz and buff, are predisposed to develop FSGS early. It is the major cause of death in elderly bucks. It would seen sensible to restrict protein and calories in adult rats unless they are nursing does. The condition is not curable but pet owners should get the condition confirmed by a vet as some life prolonging treatment is available. Treatment with the calcium compound Ipakitine or with antacids will absorb some excess phosphorus from the gut which may help to slow the disease, however Ipakitine should not be overdosed or given to rats without symptoms as some phosphorus is necessary for healthy bone growth and repair. If the condition is caught early, dietary control, including reducing protein content to 12% or less will slow the progress of the disease. These rats should not be given enrofloxacin (Baytril) or gentamicin.

3.5.4 Tumours

Urinary tract tumours seem to occur quite frequently in laboratory rats but are rare in fancy rats. Blood stained urine may be a symptom. It is probable that they are not treatable even if benign as removal may not be possible.

3.5.5 Bladderworms

The bladderworm *Trichosomoides crassicauda* is very common and is probably carried by the majority of domestic rats. They occur in the bladder, ureter and kidney of affected rats. The females are thin, hairlike and approximately 1 cm in length. The males are found inside the females. The worms are not normally seen as they live attached to the walls of the urinary tract where they release their eggs into the urine. These eggs can be seen by examining the urine under the microscope. The adult worms are only seen if they are dead or dying, possibly because they have been poisoned by something, either in the diet or by some treatment, such as ivermectin, given for another condition. The normal way a rat is infected is by its mother before weaning. The ingested eggs hatch in the babies' stomachs, then penetrate the stomach wall before going on a quick walkabout via the bloodstream and various other tissues including the lungs, eventually ending up in the urinary tract. They may cause bladder crystals and a heavy infestation of migrating larvae can cause a type of chest infection known as parasitic bronchitis. Rats with parasitic bronchitis have difficulty breathing but the condition is usually short lived although tissue scarring may occur. Otherwise the infections do not appear to cause serious problems.

Treatment, if you wish to attempt it, can be by one of the following methods. All rats should be treated at the same time:

1. 0.2% nitrofurantoin in food for six weeks
2. Single subcutaneous injection of methyridine 100mg/kg body weight
3. Ivermectin by mouth 3mg/kg body weight
4. Fenbendazole (Panacur), 0.5ml/kg by mouth for three days.

At the same time the cage should be scrubbed then thoroughly disinfected, using a disinfectant recommended for use against worm eggs (such as gluteraldehyde or 70% ethanol).

This species does not infect man.

3.6 Reproductive tract

The reproductive tract of the male rat consists of the testicles, epididymis and various glands including the prostate and preputial glands, the vas deferens and the urethra. The female reproductive tract consists of ovaries, oviducts, two horned uterus, cervix, vagina and vulva. Puberty is probably linked to weight as it appears to be in humans. This would account in part for why some rats become fertile before others. Six weeks is about average although it can happen as early as five weeks.

3.6.1 Male

The testicles of the male usually descend at about three to five weeks old and each male should have two, contained in a pouch of skin (the scrotum) between the penis and the anus. These are sometimes mistaken for a growth, as they are quite big. If only one or no testicles are seen the rat is known as a cryptorchid. This is owing to the testicles not descending. They may be present either in the abdomen or in the groin. If they are in the groin you can sometimes see them as a swelling there. If the rat is genuinely missing a testicle the rat is called a monorchid. Both of these have reduced fertility and as the condition is hereditary they should never be bred from, nor should they win stud buck classes. The testicles need to descend in order to produce sperm properly as the interior of the body is too hot. If undescended testicles are left in the body they may become cancerous, although this is probably rare and some vets will not remove them. Infertility in males is not uncommon but where a mating is unsuccessful this is normally blamed on the doe! Male infertility may be total but is more likely to involve the production of litters with low numbers of babies in them. If more than two consecutive litters from different does are small (not in the winter when smaller litters are common) it is possible that the buck is at fault. This can be due to low sperm count, poor quality sperm or the inability of the buck to stimulate the doe's ovaries to produce eggs. If a doe is mated by an infertile buck she may have a pseudopregnancy. This usually lasts 17 days. Sometimes a buck and a doe, especially when they are closely related, will not breed together, although they will breed successfully with other rats, it is therefore worth trying with other partners. Overweight bucks are sometimes not interested in sex or are unable to mount the doe properly or often enough. Occasionally old bucks may suffer atrophy of the testicles and become infertile and some varieties appear more prone to this. Male rats can pass on sexually transmitted diseases although they do not appear to be affected by them.

One infection that can cause problems is an infection of the preputial glands with *Corynebacterium kutscheri*. These glands are around the base of the penis and when infected they form small hard growths. It is not known how the organism gets there, although as it is a mouth organism it may get there during washing, but it can be treated with antibiotics, including benzyl penicillin, ampicillin, chloramphenicol and tetracycline. Baytril is not the drug of choice.

3.6.2 Female

3.6.2.1 Infertility

Females can be fertile at six weeks (five in some strains) but should not be mated before four months or until they reach a weight of 250g. Rats that are not mated before nine months stand a higher chance of infertility and if they do get pregnant a higher chance of problems during pregnancy and delivery. Although does are meant to come into season every four to six days some do not, especially if they are older or during the winter. Housing them all the time with a buck or putting some dirty sawdust from a buck's pen into the doe's cage can help. Fat does are less likely to get pregnant due to the build up of fat around the ovaries. Pregnancy rates may be low in winter (in the UK) due to the shortened hours of daylight. During the hours of darkness the pineal body in the brain secretes melatonin. In rats this can inhibit reproduction, leading to temporary infertility. It may also lead to small litters and uterine inertia due to the effect on hormone levels, although there is a lot of research still to be done in this area. It is possible to select for strains of rats which are not affected by this. Alternatively some breeders and all laboratories use lights on a 12 hour on/12 hour off cycle. Constant light will also cause infertility, something to consider if your rats live in your living room!

Rats can also absorb dead kittens in utero at almost any stage of the pregnancy. This can give the impression that a doe is not getting pregnant or has a pseudopregnancy. In rats that carry a lethal gene, for example cinnamon pearls, the homozygotes are usually absorbed before birth.

Infertility can be caused by a shortage of vitamin E and pantothenic acid (vitamin B5) although this is rare in reasonably well fed animals as they are found in whole grains. Vitamin E is added to many made up feeds. Usually rats with vitamin deficiency become pregnant but fail to carry to term.

Genetic infertility is frequently given as a cause for reproductive failure but is probably not as common as is thought. Where it occurs it tends to creep up with a history of smaller litter sizes over several generations and difficulty in getting does pregnant, whatever the time of year or age of the does.

It is also said to be caused by dichlorvos insecticide strips. However, many breeders have used these for many years without problems.

3.6.2.2 Uterine infections, metritis, pyometra

Before attempting to breed from a doe, whether or not she has had a litter before, examine her vulva for any signs of a discharge. A creamy or bloodstained discharge should stop you from breeding from her as it is a possible sign of uterine infection, usually caused by *Mycoplasma pulmonis*, although *Streptococcus pneumoniae* and *Pasteurella pneumotropica* can also cause it. These organisms can also cause snuffles and in the case of *Mycoplasma* it is thought that this infection may come from the respiratory tract via the blood stream or from the doe when she washes herself. However, most does with respiratory disease due to *Mycoplasma* do not develop uterine infections (due to the production of antibodies against it) and does with this condition frequently do not have obvious respiratory disease. It can also be sexually transmitted by the buck. If it occurs in a doe that has had a previous successful pregnancy, suspicion must fall on the buck and you should check his breeding record. If a buck has transmitted this disease, you should not use him again. If you try to mate an uninfected buck with an infected doe he will probably become a carrier in my experience. Vertical transmission, that is doe to kitten, may occur. Infection may cause infertility, abortion, small litters and dead litters. Often the only sign of an early abortion (miscarriage) is bloodstained bedding. If a litter dies *in utero* the doe may pass the litter more slowly than normal or reabsorb it. Does with this condition usually develop metritis and pyometra, indeed the discharge shows that this has probably already occurred. Breeding stock should be culled, pet animals spayed or put down. This condition is impossible to treat completely with antibiotics. If the rat is left she will steadily go downhill, losing condition and showing signs of pain before dying of the infection.

Infection with rat parvoviruses can cause absorption of embryos, small litter size, runty babies, jaundice and dead litters. The viruses attack fast growing cells including stem cells which is why embryos and young animals are more at risk. There are three strains. The most pathogenic, Kilham Rat virus, can cause severe outbreaks. This is apparently common in the United States (see *The Laboratory Rat*) but its incidence in the UK is not known although it is probably common. Any kittens which survive may suffer from jaundice or ataxia. Once a rat has had it, it becomes immune and the doe's subsequent litters are unaffected. It does not normally affect adults but when it does it can cause paralysis, encephalitis and other neurological effects. It is possibly a cause of the paralysis occasionally seen in young adults and diagnosed as encephalitis. Some breeders in the UK have experienced a run of lost litters, indicating *Mycoplasma* infection. The does have not gone on to develop metritis however and have bred successfully the second time. Testing has shown that at least some of these attacks are due to parvovirus infection. These attacks seem to occur some two to three weeks after a particular show and last two to three months. Another parvovirus, Toolan's H1, does not appear to be as pathogenic but rats do not appear to mount a good antibody response to it, meaning that they can get a chronic infection and any antibody tests to it may give a false negative result.

Another virus that has been implicated in epidemic litter loss is Sendai virus, which will also cause the birth of dead litters. However, in this case, litters are only lost if the doe is very ill with the virus. The babies do not die because they are infected but only because the doe is simply too ill to support a pregnancy.

3.6.2.3 Delivery problems

Does can go over the normal gestation period of 22/23 days due to delayed implantation of the embryos and, providing there are no signs of labour or straw coloured or bloodstained discharge, you should not worry. The signs of onset of labour in rats are:

- the bulge tends to drop from the sides to the underbelly of the doe
- the doe may develop a staring coat
- she may develop hollowing of the flanks
- some does have slightly sunken eyes
- nest building.

Signs of advanced and second stage labour are, visible muscular contractions of the abdomen and stretching followed by licking of the vulva. At all stages rats seem to be quite happy to break off and eat or investigate things!

If a straw coloured discharge is present before labour is established, or if it continues for more than a few hours there may be problems. This fluid means that the membranes around the embryos have ruptured and if it continues for too long infection can enter the uterus. It is usually a sign that the doe has developed uterine inertia. This is especially likely if the doe is running around and showing no signs of giving birth. Uterine inertia basically means that the contractions have stopped. In rats, unlike some other mammals, it is very difficult to get them started again. You have a choice here but in both cases you will probably lose the litter; you can either leave the doe or take her to the vet. If a doe looks fit and is eating and drinking well, intervention is probably unhelpful. If she is plainly unwell, however, medical intervention should be considered seriously. If you leave her she will usually pass a dead litter two to three days later. Some offspring may be left behind but she will usually absorb these without trouble. Treatment with antibiotics and fluids is helpful. The odd doe will die probably due to infection or for some underlying reason. Providing the reason for the problem was not *Mycoplasma* or some other bacterial infection she will probably be fine and give birth normally next time. If it is *Mycoplasma* she will probably be sterile and go on to develop metritis.

If you take her to the vet the normal initial treatment is an injection of oxytocin to restart the contractions. These are usually only partially successful but they can produce live offspring sometimes. The next line of treatment is a caesarean section. In the rat this usually involves a hysterectomy which means that you cannot use her for breeding any more. The litter is normally dead; for the litter to be saved the operation must be performed very early, possibly as soon as the discharge has appeared. Most does recover well from the operation but as with all operations some animals do die, especially if the vet is unused to working with rats. Although it is not recommended, some vets have chosen not to spay the doe during a caesarean, but have left the reproductive organs in place. I have known of rats to go on to have other litters successfully following this, although it is a risk.

Apart from *Mycoplasma,* the causes may be low hormone levels especially if it occurs in winter, disturbance of the doe, parvovirus infection or deficiency of vitamin A.

Does from inbred lines when outcrossed sometimes carry large numbers of big foetuses which stretch the muscles of the abdomen to the point where it is difficult for them to function properly. These does are especially likely to have a slow labour and to produce a dead litter.

A bloodstained discharge before birth can be due to a detached placenta or rupture of other membranes. If it is not heavy and stops within a few hours all may be well but sometimes this is followed by the doe aborting her litter (especially blues!). If the doe continues to bleed or the loss is heavy veterinary advice should be sought as rats cannot stand much blood loss.

Obstructed labour, that is when a doe is unable to pass a kitten even when her contractions are strong, due to the baby becoming stuck, is extremely rare. This is because the embryos are very small compared with her pelvic girdle, which means that they rarely become stuck, whatever position they present in. However, problems have occurred with big single kittens (see giant kitten syndrome 3.6.4) and in cinnamon pearls due to selection for very wide heads. If one does become stuck and you can see it, you can very carefully remove it using forceps but for most people I would recommend that you take the rat to the vet. I have to say that in 30 years of keeping rats I have only seen this a few times. If you do decide to remove the kitten yourself it is important to ease, and not pull, the kitten out.

Very occasionally you may come across a doe in labour who is in a state of collapse. This has a very bad prognosis, is possibly eclampsia and needs immediate veterinary treatment. Try giving glucose in water (with a spot of brandy in it if she is not cold) as a first aid measure and keeping her very warm. There are usually no early signs of problems. On post mortem the uterus is often full of blood, the placentas detached and degraded.

After a successful delivery, problems with the doe are rare but may involve inadequate mothering. Some does do not appear to be able to produce any milk although they may try to feed the offspring. An injection of oxytocin will usually get the milk flowing. It is not a good idea to breed with a doe like this again. Some does are just scared but can usually be encouraged to accept the babies.

Prolapse of the uterus occasionally occurs. This may be identified by the presence of a pinkish growth protruding from the vagina. It resembles, in colour and size, two chopped off pieces of earthworm stuck together and is usually about 2 cm long. It was fairly common in the first Siamese rats. The rat may appear perfectly well but nevertheless it is an emergency. Without treatment the rat will die in two or three days.

Mastitis occasionally occurs during suckling. This presents as a swollen red nipple and surrounding tissue. This is usually due to infection with *Pasteurella pneumotropica*. Treatment is usually unnecessary. If it is, care should be taken that the antibiotic chosen should not adversely affect the litter.

Litters do not normally have any serious problems until they are weaned at four to five weeks. The three that may occur are diarrhoea (wet tail), and genetic disorders including bloat and respiratory disease. These are dealt with elsewhere.

3.6.3 Red cedar sawdust

Do not use sawdust or shavings made from this tree in breeding pens. Research has shown that it is associated with high kitten mortality. The reasons are not known but is possibly due to liver toxicity. Despite some articles to the contrary, there is no good evidence that the standard bedding shavings used in the UK, which are principally from the Sitka spruce, are harmful. Indeed they are used in UK research labs and many breeders, including myself, have been using them without problems for many years.

3.6.4 Genetic and congenital disorders

These are relatively rare in well bred animals but there are some which occasionally crop up.

Cartilage hypertrophy, due to the gene, Gruneberg's lethal, occurred occasionally in the early days of the NFRS. This is a recessive condition that affects young rats at about 10 days old. Up until then they are perfectly normal but then suddenly they begin to leave the nest and wander about. Their nostrils become caked in discharge and they die in about five days. This is because the cartilage in the chest becomes solid, preventing them from breathing.

'Staggers' or ataxia also affects rats aged around 10 to 20 days. They do not walk properly but may progress diagonally or sideways, usually dragging a leg. These rats also die.

Bloat or megacolon Chinchilla rats occasionally are affected by a condition known as 'bloat'. This affects kittens at and just after weaning just as they are taking solid food. It resembles a gastrointestinal infection in that the kitten has a swollen abdomen and sometimes signs of diarrhoea. This condition is caused by a lack of nerve cells in the part of the large bowel closest to the anus. This means that the bowel is unable to function normally and the condition is similar to Hirschsprung's disease in humans. Faeces will collect upstream of this area and can lead to megacolon, a condition where the bowel becomes grossly dilated. The diarrhoea which is sometimes seen with this condition is due to the body's attempts to liquefy the blockage. This condition is congenital and is more common in the offspring of chinchillas crossed with unrelated strains, especially with hooded or other *H* mutation rats. An adult onset type also exists in these rats. In the US it also occurs in variegated and black eyed whites, however, it has not been reported in these varieties in the UK. The rate of attack is between 60% and 0%, depending on the strain. Kittens with this condition normally die within a couple of weeks. Some do survive although they are prone to bloating and alternating constipation and diarrhoea. A similar problem has been reported in adult rats following surgery. There is no cure although less seriously affected rats have been treated using Cisapride, a gut motility stimulant which has now been taken off the market due to side effects (in humans). One should be aware however that this is a painful condition and affected rats are better put down. They should never be bred from.

Giant kitten syndrome has been reported in black eyed whites, capped rats and some others. The doe gives birth to kittens one of which will be at least twice the normal size. The legs are usually the same size as in a normal kitten however and the kitten is born dead. The cause is unknown but it is thought to be inherited. However there is a condition in humans called Beckwith Wiedemann syndrome. These babies produce too much growth hormone while they are in the uterus because the gene's control mechanism has been deactivated.

Fatty or Zucker rats do occasionally crop up in strains and is due to a simple recessive gene. The condition usually appears between the third and fifth weeks of age. They are much fatter than their litter mates to the point of looking almost circular. The blood serum is milky in colour and this becomes more pronounced with age. This is due to the fact that the level of fats in the blood is up to ten times the normal. Blood sugar is normal. They are usually very greedy but will still become fat on a restricted diet. They tend not to live much over 18 months. Does have undeveloped sexual organs, including the uterus and are inevitably sterile (see photo). Bucks on the odd occasion have bred.

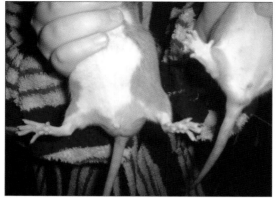

Undeveloped sex organs in a Zucker rat
(normal doe on the right)

Other conditions include kinked tails, stubby tails and tailessness, malocclusion, hydrocephalus, pug face, cryptorchidism, haemophilia, pseudohermaphroditism, missing limbs, eyes, teeth and so on. Any rat suffering from a serious condition that may be genetic or congenital should not be bred from. A strain that often produces such conditions should be discontinued.

3.6.5 Spaying and castration

Neutering male rats is sometimes used as a treatment for aggressiveness and biting in pet bucks. The operation is usually problem free and should improve temperament in three to four weeks. Vets should be aware however that the inguinal canals of rats are relatively large compared with other mammals and they remain open throughout life. These require closing off during surgery to keep the intestines in! This slightly complicates matters when compared with similar surgery in other companion animals.

An alternative to castration is to use the anti-androgen compound delmadinone acetate, marketed by Pfizer as Tardak (dosage given in the treatment section earlier 2.1.6). This compound binds with the active sites where testosterone normally attaches. This means that bucks with poor temperaments due to testosterone will be calmed by this treatment. Most rats only seem to need treatment for a few months. During this time they are not infertile but are usually uninterested in sex. However this is not a 'male pill' and should not be used as such. This drug only appears to work in those rats where castration would also be successful. Tardak should only be used for a few months and if the treatment proves successful for those few months, but when off the drug, the poor temperament returns, castration is recommended. Prolonged use may cause problems with mammary tumours. However, castration can also increase the incidence of mammary tumours in bucks as testosterone appears to have an inhibitory affect on their development.

Not all temperament problems in bucks are due to testosterone however. In such rats, these two treatments are unlikely to work. Other potential reasons are inexperienced/nervous owners, pheochromocytomas of the adrenal glands (see 3.12), or possibly some type of lesion in the brain. The use of Bach Flower remedies is recommended by some owners. There is more information under Bach Flower remedies in para 2.2.3.

40

Stud bucks may show some deterioration in temperament during their second year, especially if they have been regularly used. Providing they are not savaging does or attacking you every time you put your hand in the cage then some 'spikiness' and tooth chattering is normal if you spend too much time in their cage when they are with a doe.

Spaying female rats is only normally carried out in the UK as a treatment for metritis, uterine tumours or during a caesarean operation. In the USA in some quarters it has been recommended routinely for young pet animals to increase life span because it can prevent the growth of some types of pituitary tumour and some mammary tumours. I would not recommend this as it is known to result in bone loss if performed young and can cause pituitary tumours involving the cells responsible for producing gonadotrophic hormones. There is good evidence, however, that spaying does who have grown a fibroadenoma (the commonest type of mammary tumour in the rat) will help to prevent recurrence and conversely control those pituitary tumours which arise from those pituitary cells which produce prolactin (see tumours 3.12). Therefore by all means spay if the rat has a health condition that indicates spaying, but the evidence of the benefit of routine spaying of healthy young does is not convincing. The cost of these operations is about the same or more as that for a cat, for, while the rat is smaller, the skill required is probably greater.

3.7 Digestive tract

The rat's digestive tract consists of mouth, oesophagus, stomach, small intestine, pancreas, liver, caecum, large intestine and anus.

The rat is designed to eat small frequent meals and it has no gall bladder. It cannot vomit due to a limiting ridge of tissue in the stomach that effectively divides it. The large intestine has aspects of human and rabbit digestion. In humans the caecum and appendix are very small but large in rabbits. In rats the caecum is moderately sized. This organ is used by bacteria to help break down cellulose from plant material which mammals cannot do by themselves. The rat may absorb small amounts of breakdown products directly from the large intestine but most are reclaimed by them eating their own faeces (coprophagy). The most important nutrients they obtain this way are probably vitamin K, which is important in blood clotting, some of the B vitamins and biotin. Unlike rabbits they do not produce special droppings. Approximately 5% of their energy requirements may be obtained this way.

3.7.1 Intestinal infections and diarrhoea

3.7.1.1 Signs and symptoms

Diarrhoea in rats is not that common and can either be acute or chronic. Acute diarrhoea starts suddenly and is associated with a wet rump and vent and sometimes severe bloating and pain, dehydration is a real risk. Kittens at or just past weaning are most susceptible. Chronic diarrhoea tends to be less severe in its symptoms (loose stools, sometimes weight loss) but the rat will have those symptoms for a long time. They often show up when the rat is under stress.

Chinchilla rats, especially those with a lot of white markings, and occasionally black eyed white rats, may suffer from a congenital condition known as 'bloat'. This is due to the lack of or malfunction of some of the nerves at the end of the large intestine, causing intestinal blockages, diarrhoea and megacolon (see genetic and congenital disorders 3.6.4).

Signs of diarrhoea include wet fur around the anus, sometimes including the belly and rump. In severe cases the rat becomes pot bellied and shows signs of pain and dehydration. There may be signs of faecal staining around the rump and tail but in severe cases this will be absent and the rat can appear to have lain in a puddle of water, hence the name given in hamsters of 'wet tail'.

For a breeder acute diarrhoea in kittens is bad news as it profoundly affects growth and development.

3.7.1.2 Common causes

Reported causes are enteropathogenic *Escherichia coli, Salmonella, Clostridium piliforme (previously called Bacillus piliformis) the* cause of Tyzzer's disease, parasites such as *Spironucleus muris*, *Eimeria* sp (coccidiosis), *Cryptosporidium* and viruses such as rotavirus and reovirus 3. Chronic diarrhoea may appear only when a rat is stressed while at other times it appears normal. Sometimes the rat may have general poor health with low weight gain and poor condition. This is more likely to be due to parasites. This can be due to round worms such as *Capillaria* sp or tapeworms (*Hymenolepsis sp*). Both can be transmissible to man as are some of the bacteria, therefore cleanliness is essential. The rat pinworm, *Syphacia muris*, is very common but rarely causes diarrhoea. It can cause sticky faeces and rarely a prolapsed rectum although I have never seen or heard of this happening in a fancy rat.

3.7.1.2.1 Bacterial infections

Enteropathogenic E. coli (EPECs) are strains of *E. coli* which can attach to the cells of the small intestine, where they are believed to produce a toxin. This causes all the usual symptoms of gastrointestinal disease and it tends to attack weaners. EPECs are common causes of diarrhoea in young animals (including man) but each species has specific strains which attack them. There are very few strains which can affect more than one species. Most strains of *E. coli* are normal gut inhabitants and do not cause ill health.

Tyzzer's disease. Most rats are resistant to this disease but it can be brought about by stress and overcrowding. It is caused by an anaerobic spore forming bacterium *Clostridium piliforme*, whose usual haunt is the cells of the mammalian gut where it does not normally cause disease. The spores are very long lived and can be isolated from the soil, bedding and feed. As with EPECs the bacterium produces different strains which tend to be specific for various species. When it occurs in weaning or stressed animals the symptoms usually include staring coat, weakness, lethargy and darkening of the nail bed due to circulation failure. Death within two or three days often occurs. Diarrhoea may not be present. In older animals the symptoms tend to be more typical of gastrointestinal disease. In severe cases the liver will become infected.

Salmonellosis can be very serious in rats with a mortality of between 20 and 80%. *Salmonella* carriage by wild rats is fairly uncommon (about 1 to 5%), although those on poultry farms are more frequently infected. Recent surveys of both urban and rural rats failed to find any carriage of *Salmonella*. *Salmonella* in pet and fancy rats is probably very rare, however, animal feed can be contaminated especially with wild mouse or bird droppings. In the early part of the 20th century, cultures of *Salmonella enteritidis* var Danysz were used as rodenticides (even by Rentokil). It was even advertised as a rodenticide in *Fur and Feather* as the Danysz virus. It was fairly effective in controlling rats but it also succeeded in causing outbreaks in the human population. The World Health Organisation recommended that its use should be stopped in 1967 but it was still being used in the '80s in Italy. The reason *Salmonella* is so dangerous for rats is that it gets out of the gut and invades the body, causing enteric fever and septicaemia in them similar to typhoid (*Salmonella typhi*) in humans. The rat does not necessarily develop diarrhoea but can suffer severe anaemia and weight loss. When diarrhoea is present the faeces are soft and yellow.

Care must be taken because this organism is transmissible to humans. It is a notifiable disease meaning that all cases must be reported to the authorities. In the case of animal infections this is Defra. If a human, including yourself or a family member, catches *Salmonella* off your rats you may have problems with your local Environmental Health Department, which has to be informed of your results by the hospital pathology laboratory or your GP. The Environmental Health Department can insist that your rats are destroyed. Humans have also been known to pass salmonellosis on to rats.

3.7.1.2.2 Viral disease

Viral gastrointestinal disease in rats tends to be restricted to suckling kittens. Reovirus is a serious pathogen for mice and is believed to attack rats but not to produce such severe symptoms.

A strain of rotavirus group B causes a syndrome known as infectious diarrhoea of infant rats (IDIR). This attacks sucklings between 8 and 12 days old where it is characterised by the production of yellow diarrhoea which stains the perineum. The skin around the anus may become cracked. The rats usually survive but are often stunted in growth. Rats may shed the virus for a long time after all symptoms are gone. This virus can survive for several months out of the body.

3.7.1.2.3 Parasites

Parasites may be single celled and invisible to the naked eye (protozoa), such as *Eimeria* sp which cause coccidiosis or larger organisms, such as worms. Many of their life cycles are complex and detailed descriptions are outside the scope of this book. Therefore this is limited to the basics.

3.7.1.2.3.1 Protozoan parasites

Protozoan parasites do cause diarrhoea where they cause disease but in most cases the infection is asymptomatic. Most of the infections are self limited, that is they get better by themselves.

Coccidiosis (*Eimeria* species) can present as acute or chronic diarrhoea. It also causes weakness and weight loss over a period of weeks, and may affect the liver, although some rats will show no symptoms. It can be controlled by using rabbit feed containing the coccidiostat clopidol (Coyden), although this can be difficult to get hold of and the amount present in these pellets is insufficient to cure illness. Alternatively sulphonamides and trimethoprim/sulphonamide can be used to treat it, although in most cases this will not be necessary as it is usually self limited. It can be fatal in some cases but these rats usually have some underlying disorder. Infected rats will develop immunity but if the rat contracts a different species this immunity will not cover it, meaning that a rat can get coccidiosis more than once.

Unlike coccidiosis, *Cryptosporidium* is not completely host specific, meaning that the strain *Cryptosporidium parvum* type 2 that attacks rats can also attack other mammals including man. Animals catch it by ingesting the infective particles (oocysts) from faeces, food or water. There have been several outbreaks in humans linked to contaminated mains water supplies and if this happens in your area (this information should be released by your local water company) it is well to remember that your animals may also contract it. Symptoms are usually seen in young rats at weaning and in stressed rats following travel or overcrowding. These symptoms include lethargy, staring coat, failure to thrive and watery diarrhoea. The rat normally gets better after 10 days or so. Otherwise fit animals can carry this organism. There is no drug treatment for this infection in man or other animals. As it is transmissible to man you should be very careful, especially if you are immunosuppressed. It is a common cause of death in patients with acquired immune deficiency syndrome (AIDS).

Spironucleus muris, is quite common in a wide range of rodents and is more likely to cause disease in young and stressed animals. Infected rats show staring coats, depression, weight loss, listlessness, distended abdomen, diarrhoea and occasional death. There is no effective treatment but most rats will get better.

There are many other protozoan parasites that rats can carry but most of them do not produce disease. When they do, it is necessary to identify them in order to be sure of a diagnosis.

3.7.1.2.3.2 Worms

Roundworms. The only intestinal roundworm of the rat that you are likely to see is the rat pinworm *Syphacia muris*. This is very common and even occurs in caesarean derived laboratory stock. The worms are small, 2 to 4 mm in length and are not usually seen on the droppings. The adult females crawl out of the rat's anus to lay their eggs on the surrounding skin. Rats are infected by eating the eggs or by the newly hatched worms crawling back into the rat. If the adults are not seen, diagnosis can be made either by pressing a piece of Sellotape onto the area and transferring it to a microscope slide, or, alternatively, taking a moistened swab of the area and rubbing this gently onto a slide. The slide can then be examined under the microscope in order to find the eggs or worms. Most rats do not suffer any ill effects from their pinworm infestation although cases of prolapses of the rectum has been reported in the literature. However, I have never had any personal reports of this happening. Treatment to control worm numbers can be used if you are concerned. In studs where this infection is present, numbers of worms reach their maximum in six week old kittens. After this numbers decline as the rat develops immunity. This parasite is not transmissible to man or other livestock.

If you decide to treat then recommended treatments are piperazine citrate (such as Johnson's kitten wormer) given every day for seven days, then seven days off followed by another seven days; ivermectin, treatment on days 1-4, 8-11, 15-18 and 22-25 given at a rate of 25mg/l water (but not to pregnant or nursing does) or fenbendazole (Panacur), 150 mg/kg food dosed for alternate weeks for 21 days. At the same time it is necessary to thoroughly clean the rat's environment using a disinfectant capable of killing parasite eggs. The most effective agent is said to be 70% ethanol or methylated spirits. However, it is probably best not to treat as infection with this parasite is thought to give some protection against some types of arthritis.

Tapeworms. In comparison with the above, intestinal rat tapeworms (principally *Hymenolepsis* species) are quite big (up to 6 cm long and 0.4 cm wide for *H. diminuta*) but you are most unlikely to see the whole worm as they live in the small intestine. After the rat has fed they can move to the top of the small intestine. Tapeworms reproduce by shedding segments, each of which contain very large numbers of eggs. Tapeworm segments resemble tiny grains of rice and if fresh may be seen moving, usually on top of the faeces. Rats may get these tapeworms if they come in contact with infected wild rodents or if they eat infected fleas (including cat fleas!) or grain beetles. H. nana can reinfect the same rat directly. Infected rats usually show no symptoms of ill health although diarrhoea and poor condition are occasionally seen in heavy infestations. In rare cases the intestine may be blocked and the rat may die. The worms have a short life span and some immunity is acquired. Some rats are more susceptible than others. Treatment is with praziquantel (Droncit) which should be considered as these tapeworm species can infect humans.

3.7.1.2.3.3 Dietary change

Another cause of diarrhoea is said to be too much green food. While this does seem to affect other animals I have never seen this effect in rats and if it does occur, it is only likely to be slight and short lived. Obvious diarrhoea in the rat is usually due to an infection. However, dietary change can sometimes cause some bacteria that are normally present in the gut in low numbers to overgrow and cause symptoms. Therefore all dietary changes should be made slowly.

3.7.1.2.4 Treatment and prevention

For all diseases prevention is better than cure and prevention of intestinal infection is by good hygiene, feeding uncontaminated food and water especially in hot weather and not allowing wild animals contact with your rats' food or the rats themselves. Parasites may require an additional host in their life cycle to reproduce although some, such as Hymenolepsis, can be transmitted directly from rat to rat. Fleas are an important secondary host and therefore it is important to exclude these and treat any infestations if they occur. Exclude cats, as most cats have the odd flea and these can transmit a number of parasites to rats. Weaning rat kittens are at special risk and in addition to the above precautions you should make sure that the correct diet is fed. If the diet is unbalanced, it can make the rats more prone to disease due to an unbalanced normal gut flora.

If you decide to treat diarrhoea it is probably necessary to find out which organism is causing the disease, because the drug treatments vary with the infection. This the vet can do by sending a sample of the rat's faeces for microbiology. You should be aware however that this is expensive (even microbiologists have to eat!) and the results may take a week or so to come back. Some species, such as the Tyzzer's disease bacterium, Clostridium piliforme, do not show up on conventional culture. The most important treatment, however, in moderate to severe illness is to replace the lost fluids and prevent dehydration. This can be achieved by using a rehydration therapy available from the chemist (such as Dioralyte), Lectade from the vet or making up your own. This can be done by adding five to six teaspoons of glucose and one of common salt to 1 litre of unboiled tap water. This can be kept in the fridge up to 24 hours and then discarded. To make sure the rat drinks it you should give it 0.5 - 1ml per hour using a syringe or medicine dropper. Some people recommend the use of arrowroot biscuits or water that rice has been boiled in but I have never had much luck with these treatments. The use of over the counter anti-diarrhoea treatments should be restricted to mild formulas such as Kaopectate. Do not use Immodium (loperamide) or similar 'over the counter' treatments for human diarrhoea. They are much too powerful.

For a fancier it is better to cull animals suffering with severe diarrhoea as, if the rat survives, its growth is usually stunted and does are frequently infertile. Pets can be treated but the treatments vary with the infection. Tetracycline is normally used for Tyzzer's disease (although metronidazole, which is a superior antibiotic for this group of bacteria, should be considered). Neomycin can be helpful for those organisms such as enteropathogenic *E. coli* that remain in the gut but not for *Salmonella* which is also present elsewhere in the body. Treatment with chloramphenicol is recommended but resistance can be a problem in which case Baytril is better.

Viral conditions are self limiting and there is no effective treatment other than supportive therapy.

3.7.1.2.5 Antibiotic associated diarrhoea/colitis

Antibiotics, given for any condition, may themselves cause diarrhoea, although this is rare in rats (common in hamsters and cavies). This can be very serious and is due to the antibiotic killing off the normal gut flora and allowing dangerous enterotoxin producing species, usually *Clostridium spiroforme*, which is usually present in small numbers only, to take over. If diarrhoea starts during antibiotic treatment you should stop giving it and seek veterinary advice. Usually the diarrhoea will stop when the antibiotic is stopped. However if it continues or gets worse, treatment is difficult although probiotics and the antibiotic metronidazole may help.

3.7.1.2.6 Probiotics and prebiotics

A probiotic is a live culture of 'good' gut bacteria that are said to be able to re-colonise the intestine when it has been infected with harmful species. At the simplest, live or bio yogurts are used although their effectiveness is questionable, as the strains of the species present will not effectively colonise the rodent gut. Commercial probiotics are special mixes of bacterial cultures that can be more effective. Probiotics may help to prevent antibiotic associated diarrhoea and if you are to use one, use it after you have used the antibiotic, in case the antibiotic kills off the good bacteria as well. However, one of the commonest species used, *Enterococcus faecium*, is resistant to nearly all antibiotics anyway and therefore can be used during antibiotic treatment. While probiotics can appear to colonise an antibiotic treated gut, they are unlikely to colonise a normal gut as the resident bacterial population is likely to prevent it. Probiotics are also said to improve general health and fertility, but this has not been proven in all cases.

A prebiotic is a compound which is not digested by the animal itself but which is there to 'feed' the good gut bacteria growing in the large intestine and/or to inhibit the more pathogenic types, although things are not as simple as that. There are three groups of compounds currently being looked at: polyphenols from tea, coffee and red wine (there is a God!), transgalactosylated oligosaccharides (TOS) sometimes added to baby milk formulas and fructooligosaccharides (FOS) now being widely added to rabbit feeds (rabbits are especially prone to diarrhoeal disease). This is a hot area for research. These compounds appear to be preventative rather than curative. They are naturally present in some vegetables and fruit.

3.7.2 Liver

Liver diseases are rare in rats. Most are fatal or cause such profound health effects that most people would put affected animals down.

Tyzzer's disease, which also affects the intestine (see 3.7.1.2.1) and is caused by the bacterium *Clostridium piliforme* (previously called *Bacillus piliformis*), is characterised by a staring coat, weight loss and often sudden death. It is not necessary for the rat to have diarrhoea first. Treatment (using tetracycline) is not always possible as by the time the disease is noticed the rat is usually dead! The rat has characteristic lesions on its liver. Treatment with steroids may predispose to this condition.

Jaundice. Genetic jaundice shows up in kittens either at birth or shortly after due to a recessive gene. The affected rats show retarded growth, blood disorders and sometimes wobbly gait. A strain of laboratory rats, called Gunn rats, have a type of genetic jaundice which does not seem to affect their overall health much. I have seen jaundiced kittens and they too get over it without any ill effects.

Infective jaundice is usually caused by a rat parvovirus and also occurs shortly after birth. This virus is also associated with uterine inertia, runted and dead litters and paralysis in young adults.

Liver tumours (sarcomas) are quite big and are usually caused by the rats ingesting the eggs of the cat tapeworm *Taenia taeniaeformis*. It is untreatable but it is only likely to be contracted by rats which run around the floor where infected cats have access. If you have cats and your rats have access to the same areas you should routinely treat your cats for tapeworm and cat fleas, which transmit the tapeworm.

Liver failure in older rats has been put down to the use of sawdust and wood shavings, especially that from red cedar and some pine species. However, the evidence that these cause liver failure in rats is very poor and based on some research which shows that these beddings may cause certain liver enzymes to be raised. However there is no good evidence that raising these particular enzymes (a cytochrome p450 microsomal enzyme), even in the long term, has any negative effect on life span *or* causes liver failure in rats. Red cedar sawdust should not be used however because it has been associated with a high death rate in young kittens.

3.7.3 Pancreas

Age related type 2 diabetes mellitus is said to be common in some strains of laboratory rats including Sprague Dawleys over the age of 12 months. This can be due to endocrine system failure or possibly diet as Sprague Dawleys are very big and fat.

Diabetes in pet rats tends to occur under six months old and so is more likely to be type 1. Owners have reported that affected rats drink and urinate more frequently and tend to lose weight. They may develop an odour which has been variously described as lager, pear drops or boiling sugar. Diagnosis can be made by testing blood and urine for raised glucose levels. The condition can be treated in pet rats using insulin but requires lifelong therapy. A dosing regimen given to diabetic lab rats is as follows: 1 unit of U40 strength insulin/50g body weight per day. A unit is 0.01ml. An alternative regimen is to start treatment at 1 unit per day, increasing by 1 unit until control has been achieved. Blood sugar checks to regulate dosage will improve the accuracy of treatment. The insulin is given subcutaneously. A balanced diet is even more important than usual.

It has been postulated that as our rats have got fatter the incidence of undiagnosed type 2 diabetes has increased. This has also been linked with pododermatitis. Type 2 diabetes is best controlled by diet.

3.8 Nervous system

The nervous system consists of the brain, spinal cord (central nervous system) and the local sensory and motor nerves (peripheral nervous system).

Symptoms which may indicate problems with the nervous system include difficulties with motor function such as walking, eating, jumping, cleaning themselves and/or difficulty with sensory function such as blindness, sensitivity to light (photophobia), deafness and personality changes including nervousness, unusual docility or aggression.

3.8.1 Congenital ataxia

There are several genes that can cause problems with walking or movement in baby rats. Most times the effects are not seen until the rats are old enough to get around by themselves. Movement may be completely uncoordinated or may be crablike. These rats usually die before they are four weeks old.

3.8.2 Encephalitis/meningitis

Symptoms of these diseases include photophobia, glazed eyes, weakness in the back legs, lack of coordination, difficulty with eating, sitting hunched up and a raised temperature. In the early stages it may resemble SDAV infection, a sprained back or radiculoneuropathy. This is almost impossible to treat and once a rat is showing symptoms they usually die whatever is done. This is possibly because one of the commonest causes is rat parvovirus, which being a virus is not treatable with antibiotics. Undoubtedly some bacteria (including *Mycoplasma*) can cause this condition, in which case, treatment with the right antibiotic may help if started early enough and at a high enough dosage. It is very important that the antibiotic used can penetrate the blood/brain barrier well which quite a lot of them cannot. A good bet is chloramphenicol. This drug is restricted as in a few rare cases it can cause a type of fatal anaemia (in humans anyway!). However, as this disease is almost always a killer it is a risk worth taking. Enrofloxacin (Baytril) may also be effective. It is important that treatment continues for several days after the symptoms have gone. There have been a couple of successes, in each case, treatment started early and continued late. In the reported cases there was a high risk of the disease being passed on, therefore good quarantine is essential. If you own a number of rats it may be better to consider culling to safeguard the rest of you stock.

3.8.3 Strokes

These are normally restricted to older rats but can occur in young ones occasionally. The severity of symptoms varies. There is normally partial paralysis of the limbs on the right or left side and frequently it affects either the front or rear paw more. (Rats may have head tilt and so this condition may superficially resemble labyrinthitis.) They will have difficulty moving, sitting and eating. In severe cases the entire side may be completely paralysed. These rats should be put down. Early treatment with steroids, usually dexamethasone, (the sooner the better) can work wonders. Less severe cases may make a good recovery although you should be careful not to let them climb or fall off things. Swimming is meant to be good therapy. Homoeopathic remedies may help in which case the advice of a homoeopathic vet should be sought, however, the use of Arnica as a first aid measure can be useful.

3.8.4 Pituitary and other brain tumours

Benign pituitary tumours (nearly always adenomas) are said to be the second most common form of tumour in older female rats. The symptoms of a large tumour include loss of coordination, lethargy, head tilt, weight loss and porphyrin tinged nasal discharge. It is more common in rats which are overfed. Symptoms of small or microadenomas are more subtle and are linked to the hormones they are secreting. Pituitary tumours arise in specific cell types in the pituitary and the hormone secreted depends on the cell type. The most common pituitary tumour in the rat arises from a group of cells called mammotrophs which secrete prolactin. Raised levels of this hormone is linked with mammary tumours (see tumours 3.12). Treatment can be attempted with tamoxifen, bromocryptine or Cabergoline. Steroid treatments, for instance using dexamethasone, can help reduce inflammation and prolong life. However the side effects can be severe and include abscesses often caused by *Corynebacterium kutscheri*.

Other brain tumours or abnormalities in the brain which take up space (space occupying lesions) such as blood clots and abscesses, may produce a similar range of symptoms to the above including loss of coordination, personality changes, photophobia, head tilt, epilepsy and stiffened legs. There is no treatment but steroids may prolong life a short time, however I would recommend that the rat is put down.

3.8.5 Fits

Fits, usually epilepsy, are rare but may range from sudden stillness and inattention, where the rat does not appear to be aware of its surroundings, to severe symptoms involving unconsciousness, thrashing about and severe tremors. Death may occur during severe fits and almost as seriously the rat may bite through its tongue! As they don't appear to be able to get their teeth out again, the tongue may swell to such an extent that the rat chokes before it can be helped. Sudden loud noises or movements may spark off an attack. Attacks caused by loud noises are called audiogenic seizures and are inherited as a threshold trait. The research is reviewed in *Genetics of the Norway Rat* by Roy Robinson. This occurs in black-eyed white rats. Treatment to control the fitting using the sedative phenobarbitol can be successful.

3.9 Fur and skin

3.9.1 Baldness (alopecia)

Once a kitten has grown a complete fur coat, it should maintain this all its life. Thin coats and baldness are not normal in rats (except for hairless rats and rexes). Rats are covered with fur or bristles all over except for the palms and soles of the feet. Rats also have tactile hairs all over their coat. These are important in helping rats form a picture of their environment, especially in the dark. This sense of touch may also be important in the rats' personal relationships.

3.9.1.1 Genetic baldness/sphynx rats

Rats homozygous for the rex gene (*Re*) may be bald. These are sometimes called double rexes by fanciers because they have two copies of the rex mutant gene. Most show rexes are heterozygous, that is they have one copy. When the rats are homozygous the coat grows through and then breaks off. Some older heterozygous rex males get a thin coat along the back. Keeping the rat's weight controlled can stop the worst effects. As the rat gets fatter the coat will look thinner due to the stretching of the skin. However, rats with a thinning coat seem to be more prone to lay down subcutaneous fat. Apart from this rex mutation there are at least seven other mutations that can cause hairlessness in rats. The fur usually grows through and then breaks off. Some of these genes cause early death and ill health.

3.9.1.2 Barbering

Some rats chew other rats' coats and occasionally the whiskers as well. This is called barbering. In bucks this chewing usually shows up as a lack of guard hairs on the sides. It is more obvious in the ticked varieties such as cinnamon pearls and agoutis. In does guard hair loss is chiefly seen on the shoulders, neck and cheeks and in some cases may lead to completely bald patches and include loss of the whiskers. In both bucks and does this chewing is usually performed by a dominant animal to a submissive one, however it is likely that barbering is hereditary. Discovering the barberer is easy, it is the rat that has not been chewed! Unless of course you have two. Some does do not chew other rats but chew the fur on their own forelegs, armpits or groin. These are more likely to be submissive rats. All rats that barber should not be bred from. However, barbering is said to be commoner in rats on a high fat diet.

Barbered rats may take some months to regrow a complete coat.

3.9.2 Thin coats

Thin coats can be caused by vitamin and mineral deficiency and if you suspect this then you should seek to improve the diet. If you decide to use a supplement, make sure that you choose one that includes the necessary levels of vitamins and trace minerals. It is not true that these supplements can do no harm. Most feeds contain added A and D vitamins. If the rat is also fed a supplement they may become overdosed with vitamin A.

Lack of biotin can cause baldness that starts as spectacles around the eyes and then spreads to the back and shoulders. It may also cause lack of pigment and thus resemble copper deficiency. Biotin deficiency is rare as it is normally supplied by the intestinal microflora and recovered when the rat eats its faeces. However, intestinal upsets or antibiotic treatment may induce deficiency. It is normally present in good quality supplements.

Does with litters sometimes have thin coats. This should improve however within a few weeks. Selection for a short coat in show rats can lead to rats having thin coats on the belly (meaning you can see the skin through the fur). This is a fault and should be watched for as judges will fail rats for it. Old rats often develop thin coats, this can mean that they are unable to get all they need out of their diet and may need a supplement.

Endocrine disease, such as an underactive thyroid and Cushing's syndrome can also cause thinning of the coat.

3.9.3 Pigment loss

The most common place to see pigment loss is around the eyes, occasionally spreading on to the shoulders. This, when combined with progressive baldness in these areas could be due to biotin deficiency. When not combined with baldness, copper deficiency is more likely. Copper deficiency is quite common in rats fed an exclusive diet of processed food which has less than 10mg/kg of diet (15mg/kg of diet is recommended).

Feed a good quality vitamin/mineral supplement. Treatment with the androgen suppressant Tardak may cause pigment loss.

3.9.4 Spots and scabs/pruritus/protein itch/mange

These are small scabs that appear on the shoulders, neck, head and chin. They are caused by the rat scratching itself with its back claws due to skin irritation, known as pruritus. It is a characteristic of this condition that it usually affects a limited number of rats and often only one rat in a cage will have it. It is commoner in subordinate rats (especially bucks), pregnant and nursing females and any other rat suffering stress. Histological examination of skin biopsies tends to show a non specific inflammatory response. The irritation is usually due to a reaction (probably allergic) to items in the diet or more commonly mites (see below). Secondary infection of the scratches with *Staphylococcus aureus* may complicate treatment. When this occurs the scratches appear reddened and may weep pus. *Staphylococcus aureus* may also cause an impetigo-like syndrome in young rats. In this case patches of yellowish crusting with associated hair loss will occur, usually on the back or shoulders. This is self limiting but can be treated with tea tree oil, Hibiscrub or Fucidin cream. Care should be taken as it is transmissible to humans.

More rarely pruritus can be due to ringworm or an allergy to the bedding.

3.9.4.1 Mites

There are several species of mite that may be responsible for scabs and skin irritation, but *Notoedres muris*, the ear mange mite, is probably not one of them as this is specifically said to cause ear mange. The mite species which may be responsible could be *Radfordia ensiferi*, the rat fur mite, although this species does not burrow, or *Demodex* species, a genus of burrowing follicular mite quite commonly found on rats and often said to be nonpathogenic. *Myobia musculi* and *Mycoptes musculinus* which infect mice may occasionally be found. The fur mite, *Radfordia ensifera,* can be seen in the coat and especially behind the ears. They resemble small white dots. *Demodex* mites are not visible. Mites can be examined by using Sellotape slides (for *Radfordia*), and skin scrapings or hair follicles (for *Demodex*). The irritation is probably due to an allergic response to the mites or their waste products. Where rats get their mites from is a bone of contention. Mites normally stay on their host unless that animal dies, at which point they will leave if they can. Some species can survive up to three weeks off a rat, although the eggs can survive much longer. Mites will pass from one rat to another by direct contact, although some people consider that hay is a risk factor and should not be used. However, most rats carry a few mites without symptoms and it is probable that affected rats have not 'caught' their mites recently at all. There doesn't seem to be any link between mite numbers and disease. Not all rats produce the same reaction. Rats in colonies where mite infection is widespread (nearly all fancy and pet colonies) become infected via their mother. However, healthy rats slowly become immune and as they do mite numbers begin to decrease when the rats are two to three months old. Clinically apparent mite infection occurs in debilitated or chronically diseased rats, rats housed in stressful environments, pregnant or nursing animals, rats moving down the pecking order and so on. This may be due to variations in grooming behaviour or altered immune response.

Prevention, by using a dichlorvos fly strip such as a Vapona in the shed is very effective but they are now difficult to obtain. Affected individuals should first have their back claws clipped to stop them damaging themselves further. This is important even if you think that the nails are short. After this they can be treated with ivermectin (Ivomec) or fipronil (Frontline). Ivermectin can be given either by mouth or by injection or by placing a small drop behind the ears. Be careful when using these compounds as they can be toxic and may have accumulative affects. Ivermectin should not be used on pregnant, nursing or very young stock. Permethrin dusting powder is sometimes recommended in text books but I have never had any luck with it. It needs to be repeated weekly and the cages treated as well as the rats. Johnson's Anti-mite Spray can be used but may cause breathlessness in some rats. Sulphur homoeopathic remedy may help once the mites have been controlled. In my opinion rats that suffer badly from this condition should not be bred from as the tendency to react this badly is hereditary.

Another mite, the tropical rat mite, *Ornithonyssus (Liponyssus) bacoti*, is sometimes mentioned in text books. Unlike the other species which live on skin or its secretions this is a blood sucking parasite and heavy infestations will cause anaemia and even death. It normally lives on the bedding and is bigger than the other species. It also bites man! I have not heard any reports regarding outbreaks in the UK. If you get this mite in the house you may have to call in a pest control company as it is very difficult to destroy in that situation.

3.9.4.2 Diet

Sunflower seeds and peanuts can cause skin irritation and they should be restricted to treats only, no more than four to five seeds per day each. They have no special food value for rats and while they love them their fat concentration is too high. It is not known what element in these foods causes the problem. It has also been associated with some corn products.

This condition is sometimes called protein itch. However, there is no evidence that rats fed high protein diets have a higher incidence of skin irritation.

3.9.5 Lice

The spined rat louse *Polyplax spinulosum* is frequently not recognised by owners and infested rats often turn up on the show bench. This louse is about 0.5 -1.5mm in length and yellow brown in colour. It is said to move slowly (unlike the human head louse) although the ones I have seen have not been at all slow on their feet unless they are feeding. It is not transmissible to man. Normally it is the eggs (nits) that are noticed. These are 0.2mm in length, oval and fastened securely to the hairs. They are brown before hatching but white afterwards. They are most noticeable on the fur of the rump but rats with a slight infestation can be hard to spot. The lice themselves can be anywhere but the groin appears the most favourable place. The feeding lice (which don't appear to move at all) can be seen attached to the underside of baby rats before they get their fur. They will leave a small round bite mark that you can spot with practice. Lice are blood sucking parasites and severe infestation can cause spots and a general unthrifty appearance. Lice can carry several diseases to rats including the blood infection haemobartonellosis. In susceptible rats this causes severe anaemia. Treatment for lice is with ivermectin, Frontline and human antilouse preparations. These cannot be used on baby rats, pregnant or nursing does. Dichlorvos strips will also control infestation and if you have more than a few rats this is the most effective form of treatment, however now this is not for sale in the UK and needs to be bought over the internet. Once the eggs are attached you will have to wait until the rat moults out to get rid of them as they are firmly cemented on to the hair. A nit or flea comb does not work on rat fur.

3.9.6 Fleas

Fleas are rare on fancy rats but are common on wild ones! In the UK the flea that attacks rats the most is the Northern rat flea *Nosopsyllus fasciatus*. This will bite humans if it can't get rat. Treatment is the exclusion of wild rats and regular and thorough changes of bedding as fleas breed in this. In sheds the floor must also be properly and thoroughly swept and in the house, carpets etc thoroughly vacuumed. Drug treatments are not necessary. They can transmit rat tapeworms.

Cat fleas, *Ctenocephalides felis*, will attack rats and in addition can carry several diseases. Good flea control of any cats is important if you also have rats.

3.9.7 Bites and abscesses

Rat bites normally involve the skin only and, providing the underlying tissues are undamaged, they will normally heal without incident. I must add that these bites look bad as you can see the muscles but they really are superficial. Even the very long slashes of 2 to 3 cm should not be sutured, although you can use some wound powder or saline spray if you wish. Stabbing bites, into the underlying tissues occasionally prove fatal if they pierce a major blood vessel. Sometimes deep bites will form abscesses due to wound infection, either with the bacteria already on the rat's skin or from the bacteria on the other rat's teeth. An abscess is a pocket of infection that becomes walled off from the rest of the body by a protective response of the animal's immune system. Normally an abscess comes to a head as a large painful lump at the site of an old wound and bursts out onto the surface, draining the pus and bacteria away. You can help this process by bathing it in warm water. Sometimes people are advised to lance abscesses but normally it will burst itself. If it is necessary to lance one it should be done at the lowest part of the abscess in order to let all the pus drain away by gravity and to help prevent any more from accumulating. The cut should be large enough and left uncovered and unsutured. Cleaning with dilute hydrogen peroxide or saline will remove some of the pus and the cavity can be treated with wound powder. If the abscess heals over without draining properly it will recur or it may form a sinus. Deep abscesses, or those which rupture internally can cause peritonitis, septicaemia or pleurisy depending on where they are situated. This is usually fatal. Abscesses which occur on the tail root or the perineum are serious because these may extend into the spinal canal. These require veterinary advice.

Some people advise treatment with a systemic antibiotic after surgery to kill any bacteria that may get into the body. However, the best way of using them is to start treatment an hour or two *before* the abscess is lanced, so that there are adequate amounts in the blood before the organisms get there. Rats on long-term steroid treatment may develop multiple abscesses due to *Corynebacterium kutscheri*. These are unlikely to clear up while the rats are on the treatment, although antibiotics can help to control the infections. *Corynebacterium* abscesses are characteristic as they are filled with a material resembling cream cheese.

Deaths from most abscesses, even without any treatment, are rare. The exceptions are tooth abscesses, which although exceedingly rare are often fatal, and those that affect the spinal canal or brain.

3.9.8 Ringworm

This is a contagious fungal infection of the skin and hair. It is relatively rare in rats but when it occurs it causes patches of clumped fur leading to hairlessness (usually but not always ovoid in shape) normally over the back. Unlike barbering, however, the skin is usually roughened or scaly within the patch. Ringworm in rats is either caused by *Microsporum* species or by *Trichophyton mentagrophytes*. Diagnosis is confirmed by examining skin scrapings treated with 10% potassium hydroxide under the microscope. Some vets like to use a long wavelength (365nm) ultraviolet light called a Wood's lamp as some species of fungi will fluoresce when viewed this way. This test is of limited use however as *Trichophyton* species never fluoresce and not all *Microsporum* species will. The infection may clear up by itself. Treatment in animals with fur is with griseofulvin or ketoconazole by mouth or alternatively dipping in Imaverol (enilconazole) or applying topical ointment such as Daktarin Gold or Nizoral, and may take several weeks. These fungi will also cause ringworm in humans. Cages of infected rats can be scrubbed using an iodine containing disinfectant such as Vanodine 18 or Betadine. Impetigo, caused by *Staphylococcus aureus*, may produce similar symptoms. Both conditions are more common in rats kept in crowded conditions.

3.9.9 Greasy coats

Bucks sometimes have very greasy areas of coat, especially in the middle of the back. This can give rise to skin problems. It is caused by bucks (especially fat ones) not being able to groom their backs properly. It normally occurs only in bucks kept by themselves and virtually never in those housed with does. Washing or the use of a dry powder shampoo can be attempted but may make the problem worse. Some owners have recommended the use of Swarfega to wash these rats. Castrated rats are also said to suffer less. My opinion is that this is chiefly a husbandry problem and yet another reason for not keeping rats by themselves.

Deficiency of some B vitamins may cause greasy coats but in this case the greasiness is more widespread and can occur in both sexes.

3.9.10 Brown skin

Adult bucks characteristically have a layer of brown skin on the back and shoulders. This is due to oxidised sebaceous secretions and is testosterone enhanced. It is perfectly normal but can be washed out if you wish. Occasionally some does may have this, presumably ones with raised testosterone levels.

3.10 Feet and tail

3.10.1 Sore heels/hocks, bumblefoot, ulcerative pododermatitis

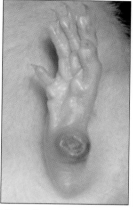

Deb Mallett

Ulcerative pododermatitis

Overweight rats may develop sores on the hind feet where the heel would be in a human or the hock on a horse (in rodents this is the tarsal joint). I have never seen this in a stud buck or any other rat in a breeder's establishment that was not overweight. It was traditionally linked with cages with wire floors but these have not been in general use for about 30 years. Some people believe that shavings are to blame but if this was the case then this condition would be common in breeder's establishments which it isn't. In fact it is extremely rare. There is good evidence that the condition tends to be hereditary so do not breed from sufferers. Some research indicates a link to type 2 diabetes.

It first resembles a small lump but this quickly develops into a raw sore area. It is a type of pressure sore and appears to be commoner in fat, lazy rats sitting about, often in cardboard or plastic boxes and urinating where they sit like a sort of rodent couch potato. It is uncommon in females, possibly due to their more active lifestyle. Once established this is a difficult condition to treat and complete cure is extremely rare. This is shown by the large number of available treatments. The following is a basic method that has proved helpful.

Encourage the rat to take more exercise, remove cardboard and plastic boxes, clean shelves and platforms daily, make sure that there is a good layer of clean bedding on the floor of the cage, put the rat on a diet and treat the feet with a dry wound powder or purple spray for horses (equivalent to blue lotion or blue kote sold in the US) twice a day. However, be careful not to knock off any formed scabs. Alternative bedding is Vetbed which can be washed and reused many times. Do not use tissues or paper. These concentrate the urine in that area and allow it back onto the rat's feet. Good quality hay or straw can be used as this tends to drain the urine away from the rat's feet. Surgical removal of scar tissue is rarely successful.

Use of a topical antibiotic cream to control the inevitable secondary infections may be indicated. The infection is usually *Staphylococcus aureus* but other organisms may be implicated.

As an alternative to the veterinary wound powder applying a plaster dressing may allow the feet time to heal and some people have had good results using tea tree oil. This should be applied every few days and held in place with the dressing. Do not be tempted to change the dressing too often as this will damage the healing tissue.

NFRS member Rachel Rodham had success with the following method:

Mix crushed comfrey leaves with vegetable oil in a jam jar and put the jar in a pan of simmering water. Leave for quite a long time until the liquid is dark green. Strain, add tea tree oil and essential oil of lavender. Soak a small piece of cotton wool in this and strap on to the foot with plaster. Replace every couple of days. The extract will last for some time. Store in the fridge. However, be careful not to contaminate it and only dip in sterile cotton wool or sterilised equipment. Keep fingers out.

Homoeopathic Silicea and Hypercal cream has also been recommended. All treatment needs to be continued for some weeks or months.

3.10.2 Foot injuries

Bites to the feet should be treated carefully with antiseptic powder as they commonly become infected. Infections of the feet sometimes lead to septic arthritis. Toe nails sometimes get pulled out. These bleed profusely but treatment apart from wound powder is unnecessary.

Toes and fingers sometimes become broken. These are too small to be set but will heal without treatment. Warts caused by a papilloma virus sometimes appear on the feet. These look nasty and are contagious. However the condition is self limiting.

3.10.3 Foot and mouth disease

This devastating disease of livestock has been included here because in the UK outbreak of 2001 there were implications for the rat fancy and much conflicting information, including some from official bodies.

According to research carried out at the Animal Virus Research Institute, Pirbright, Surrey, rats can contract FMD by eating infected material and they can carry and transmit the virus for several months. However they do not develop symptoms unless the virus is directly injected into the footpad, when they may develop a few pustules on the feet. They cannot get the virus by the airborne route. Unless a rat is in direct contact with an infected animal it is not at risk either of getting the disease or carrying it.

3.10.4 Tail injuries

Tail injuries caused by skinning (the skin of the tail coming off) are rarer in rats than in mice but sometimes occur due to fights, accidents or poor handling. The resulting raw area of bone and tissue can safely be left as it soon dries up and falls off or is removed by the rat. This process normally takes about one week. The tail cannot regrow except when small lengths of tail are lost by small kittens. If it starts to cause pain or becomes infected it should be amputated.

Tails rarely become broken. If the portion below the break is limp then this should be removed, as otherwise it will become damaged and infected.

Damage to the tail root caused by falls and poor handling have been reported. In these cases the tail appears to be bent to one side and can be painful. Sometimes the tail is bowed in an S shape, due to the uneven pulling of the ligaments. The tail does not improve in position but usually ceases to bother the rat. Open exercise wheels may also cause tail injuries.

3.10.5 Ringtail

Ringtail is the development of one or more rings of swelling and inflammation around the tail which can cause the portion of the tail after the ring to drop off. It occurs in unweaned rats between 7 and 15 days old that are housed where the relative humidity is under 20%. High and low temperatures, deficiencies in fatty acids and occasionally widespread infection have also been linked with this condition. It is thought to be due to a faulty response of the temperature regulation blood vessels in the tail.

Ringtail rarely occurs in the UK except occasionally in inadequately humidified air conditioned breeder units. This is because the relative humidity in the UK hardly ever drops below 40%. The use of wire bottomed cages with cat litter bedding which soaks up all the moisture predisposes to this condition. If the condition is caught early enough (before the tail drops off) then tail damage can be prevented by increasing the local humidity using wet towels and so on.

3.10.6 Kinked tails

A kinked tail is a sharp bend in the tail due to a misplaced joint. They are usually quite small and found near the tip of the tail. Most kinks are congenital, that is the rat is born with it. They are also hereditary, but as most of them are very small they are quite often not noticed by the judges. It is very difficult to kink a rat's tail by shutting it in a cage door. It is not uncommon for an exhibitor to tell a judge that a rat did not have a kink in the morning. However, if the kink had been due to an accident then there would be considerable bruising and damage to the area concerned. There are no health implications and no treatment.

3.11 Skeleton

3.11.1 Broken bones

A broken back is of course untreatable and the rat should be put down as soon as possible. The rat's hind legs and tail will be completely limp and paralysed. However, this can also occur if the back has sustained less serious damage. Under these circumstances the symptoms may improve. An X-ray is worthwhile. In the case of less serious damage an injection of steroid such as dexamethasone as soon as possible after the accident has been shown to be helpful in humans. You could also try the homoeopathic remedy Arnica, which is said to be helpful for treating inflammation.

The treatment given for broken long bones in the legs depends on the health of the rat, type and position of the break, the skill of the vet and cost! They may be left to heal by themselves, amputated, splinted or pinned internally.

Most vets would recommend that the bone was left to set by itself, by enclosing the rat in a small cage where it cannot climb. Bones do set by themselves but may not set straight and will be very painful for some time. The use of a pain killer is recommended. Some clinicians are unwilling to use pain killers on rats because they consider that the rat then may be encouraged to do too much. However, the use of some pain relief, especially if the rat seems depressed, is helpful. In the two cases of broken bones I have seen the fracture was a compound one with the bones protruding through the skin. In such a case infection would be a major hazard and leaving the break may not be an option. Amputation may be a better bet.

External splinting is not generally used much because the rat would have to wear a collar for some time in order to prevent it removing the splint. This procedure is described in *Handbook of Rodent and Rabbit Medicine,* see bibliography.

Some vets will pin fractures internally. This takes a lot of skill and is usually very expensive. It is not suitable for all fractures although where it is possible it can produce a better result.

In most cases fractures heal in about three weeks.

Tails also get broken occasionally and may require amputation.

3.11.2 Arthritis

There are several types of arthritis but the two most common in rats are osteoarthritis; suffered by old rats, and septic arthritis which is commoner in young rats. Rats over two years old sometimes suffer from stiff and swollen joints due to osteoarthritis. This is caused by the joint linings wearing away so that bone rubs on bone causing an overgrowth of bony tissue and a lot of pain. These rats should be kept warm and care should be taken when they exercise as they are more likely to fall. Aspirin can be given safely to rats (for the dosage see treatments 2.1.4). This is useful for arthritis because it relieves swelling and pain.

Septic arthritis, sometimes called foot-rot, is commoner in mice than in rats. There are several bacteria responsible. The commonest one in rats is *Mycoplasma arthrididis*. *Streptobacillus moniliformis, Staphylococcus aureus* and *Corynebacterium kutscheri* can also cause this. It is normally caused by a bite to the feet from another rat as the organisms usually live in the mouth of the rat, although it can follow pododermatitis or *C. kutscheri* respiratory infection. *St moniliformis* can also cause rat bite fever in humans. Septic arthritis normally affects the joint closest to the bite. The joint becomes swollen, red and painful. The rat often sits huddled up. After a day or so a hole appears and pus leaks out. Without antibiotic treatment the animal slowly deteriorates, as the infection does not clear up and often spreads to other joints. As good penetration is necessary and as it is not normally known which organism is to blame I would recommend enrofloxacin (Baytril) although generally I believe that the use of this drug should be restricted to all but the most serious cases. I have heard of a rat with this who had its foot amputated but this is recommended for only the most intractable cases!

3.11.3 Lack of coordination and paralysis

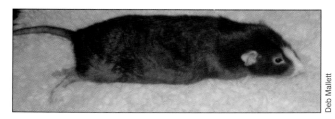

Rat with hind leg paralysis

Radiculoneuropathy is a condition in rats over two years old where the hindquarters become progressively more weak, floppy and paralysed. It appears to be due to progressive degeneration of the spinal nerve roots. It is more common in bucks. There is no cure but as this condition appears linked to age related kidney failure, treatment with Ipakitine to control this can also help with the paralysis (see kidney failure 3.5.3). Other forms of rear end paralysis can be due to encephalitis due to infection with parvovirus etc (in younger rats) and accidents such as falls. Brain and pituitary tumours will also cause loss of coordination and general unsteadiness. Most conditions are generally chronic and if the rat is to be kept alive, it will require careful handling and management. All shelves should be removed from the cage to prevent falls and care should be taken that the rat is able to feed and clean itself.

3.12 Tumours

Doe with two tumours

Contrary to what you can read in some books on pet rats, most tumours in rats are not cancerous but benign. They tend to occur in rats over 18 months of age and are linked with age related changes in endocrine function. According to most surveys of laboratory strains the commonest tumours are mammary fibroadenomas, pituitary adenomas (specifically prolactinomas, see pituitary tumours 3.8.4) and an adrenal gland tumour called a pheochromocytoma. In many cases rats with mammary fibroadenomas also have a preexisting prolactinoma, which appears to encourage mammary tumour growth. A review of the research looking into these tumours is published by the NFRS and is listed in the bibliography.

The most common tumours in rats are benign mammary fibroadenomas. These are found under the front legs, in the groin, behind the nipples, on the belly and up the flanks as the mammary tissue is widespread in the rat. These tumours are mostly found in does but can occur in bucks as these too have some mammary tissue. The use of both Tardak (to control testosterone linked aggression) and castration can predispose to mammary tumours in bucks as testosterone appears to be a preventative. Although these can get very large (bigger than the rat) they can normally be removed satisfactorily. They quite commonly recur at another site however (especially in rats who also have prolactinomas). Mammary fibroadenomas may become dangerous if they become infected or become so large that they press on the rat's internal organs. They are much commoner in fat rats than ones that are the correct weight. These tumours can sometimes be treated with tamoxifen (1mg/rat daily but not all will take it), and as they are frequently associated with a small pituitary prolactin producing tumour, with

59

bromocryptine. This drug is used to treat prolactinomas in humans and has been widely studied in laboratory rats. Alternatively spaying a rat with a mammary or pituitary tumour often proves effective as it removes most of the oestrogen, which is important in the growth and development of some of these tumours. Routine spaying of young rats to stop these tumours growing in the first place is dubious, as it may predispose to other types of pituitary tumours and to osteoporosis. Occasionally a more dangerous cancerous tumour may occur in this site.

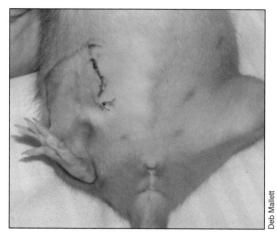

Operation site following a successful tumour removal

Pheochromocytomas are tumours found in the medulla of the adrenal glands in a number of mammals including rats. Surveys in laboratory rats have put the incidence at between 86% and 12% among males; it is rare in females. The medulla produces adrenalin and noradrenalin, the flight or fight hormones. Pheochromocytomas secrete noradrenalin and in humans they induce headache, sweating and nervousness, especially during stress but I could not find any reference to the symptoms in rats. However, as the effect of this hormone is to raise blood pressure by vasoconstriction, it is possible that some of these middle aged bucks which suddenly become prone to poor temperament, especially at shows, could be suffering from this tumour. Rats and other animals with this tumour have raised levels of these hormones and their metabolites in their urine

Cancerous tumours usually come up in a matter of days in rats and can kill in less than a month. They can be found in nearly any place and at any age although they are commoner in younger rats. Surgery may successfully remove the tumour but rapid re-growth is common. Metastases (that is secondary tumours) are very rare in rats. Cancers in rats are well covered in the book *The Laboratory Rat* (see bibliography). One of the commoner ones, histiocytic sarcoma, produces widespread diffuse disease and is always fatal.

3.12.1 Prevention

For the breeder, lines of rats that consistently produce tumours should be discontinued. Much of the blame for the incidence of tumours in rats has been laid at the feet of tumour prone laboratory stock although most of the fancy stock in the UK did not arise wholly from laboratory lines but from the pet and fancy lines that survived between the 1920s and the 1970s. However, lab stock has been introduced into the fancy fairly frequently in the shape of the rex, Siamese and the topaz, as well as a lot of pink eyed whites, however, most lines of laboratory rats have not been selected to grow tumours. In Germany, which seems to have a special problem, crossing with wild rats has been attempted but this has not decreased tumour incidence. Indeed surveys of wild rats have found a similar range of tumours to that in laboratory strains although the incidence was lower. However, the ages of the wild rats were not known and as wild rats rarely live beyond one year, this incidence may be incorrect.

More important than the breeding is husbandry, especially diet. Rats fed high calorie, high fat diets *ad lib* are more likely to develop tumours than those fed more restricted diets. Rats should not be allowed to become overweight and it is not necessary to have food present all the time. Viewed from above a rat should resemble a tube and not a potato. Feed adults a 50:50 mix of commercial rat diet and 14% protein rabbit mix. Add fruit and vegetables and the odd cooked chicken bone. A good quality vitamin and mineral supplement, containing selenium and copper, should also be fed. Remove uneaten perishable food every day but the dried food should be completely eaten before any more is offered. The diets of young and nursing rats should not be restricted however.

3.13 Hypothermia

This occurs when a rat's body temperature drops more than a few degrees below normal (99.5°F, 37.5°C). The rat becomes progressively more lethargic and cold to the touch. The coat stares, the eyes appear sunken and the ears are carried flat to the head. Eventually the rat becomes unconscious and dies. If the rat is still conscious, put it in a warm place in a box of bedding, in front of a fire or radiator. Alternatively tuck it inside your jumper. Give it a warm drink when it comes round. If it is unconscious you will have to do something pretty drastic to save it. The only way I have found of doing this is again to put it somewhere warm, but also to get it to swallow some brandy by using a pipette and rubbing its throat. This is frowned on by the medical profession but the slowly, slowly approach does not work with severely hypothermic rats. This condition usually only occurs in young rats that get damp and cold. I have seen it happen when a water bottle has leaked in the winter. Providing that the rats are given plenty of dry bedding and good, high calorie food, cold does not affect them as much as heat does. As hypothermia can strike quickly you should keep your eyes open for this condition. Treated rats usually make a quick and complete recovery. Hypothermia can follow surgery.

3.14 Heat stroke or hyperthermia

This occurs when the rat is unable to keep its temperature down to normal limits, usually due to excessively hot surroundings. The rat lies down, becomes limp, pants and the eyes become wide and staring. The ears often appear very red. It is commoner in bucks than does and is liable to happen whenever the temperature of the rat's surroundings goes above 85°F, 30°C. It can also happen following anaesthesia. Sudden rises in temperature are more dangerous than gradual ones.

Sponge the rat down using cool water and put him in a cool, dark place. As soon as he will take it, give him water with salt added (one teaspoon to 1 litre). Do not pull him around or handle him unnecessarily. Some rats appear to recover only to die later, possibly from heart or kidney failure.

Care should be taken to keep sheds and rat rooms cool in summer by leaving doors and windows open and insulating the shed roof especially. Make sure that the rats are getting enough water although this will not by itself prevent heat stroke. When you take rats to shows in hot weather, leave the big bucks at home and make sure that the others have plenty of ventilation. Do not leave them for long in parked cars! Take a water spray with you and spray them after judging has finished. Never house rats in conservatories, porches or opposite unshaded windows.

4 VITAMINS AND MINERALS

The bulk of a rat's daily vitamin and mineral requirements should be freely available in the normal diet, providing you feed properly although storage may decrease vitamin but not mineral content. The amounts of vitamins and minerals obtained by feeding grains and vegetables is variable and dependent on the soil they have been grown in, the time since harvesting and the way they have been stored. Frozen vegetables frequently have higher vitamin content than fresh. Some vitamins, especially vitamin K, which are available in only low amounts in the diet, are made by the bacteria in the rats' gut and the rats get them by eating their droppings (coprophagy) or absorbing the vitamin directly from the intestine. They also obtain extra biotin, some B vitamins and folates by this method. Rats, like most other mammals, make their own vitamin C and therefore do not require it in their diet.

The use of a vitamin and mineral supplement can be useful to provide for any lack, but please remember that excess of some, especially vitamin A, can be dangerous, especially because some are also added to many feeds. Before using a supplement check which vitamins and minerals it contains and in what amounts. Ensure it is not past the use by date and store in a cool dry place.

Shortage of vitamins can cause many symptoms, depending on the ones that are lacking. Commonest symptoms are sparse or dull coat, poor growth and litter loss. In severe cases death can result but this is most unlikely.

Some minerals are necessary in such tiny amounts that unless an animal is living in an environment that specifically excludes it, the rat is most unlikely to become deficient. This includes nickel, vanadium, silicon and tin. In addition some others such as sodium, potassium and sulphur are so common in foods that deficiency is unlikely unless the rat becomes dehydrated. Zinc is present in galvanised cage bars, so that rats kept in cages with bars made of this will need less in their diet because they will obtain some of the zinc that they need by chewing the bars. For further information regarding these elements I would recommend *The Laboratory Rat*.

Tables A and B list vitamins and minerals which may conceivably be lacking and their deficiency symptoms.

Table A – Vitamins

Vitamin	Natural source	Essential for	Deficiency causes
A (Retinol)	Green, yellow and red vegetables and fruit as beta carotene, dairy produce, liver. *Added to most feed*	Normal growth and repair of tissues vision, resistance to infection	Poor growth, thickening and roughening of skin and mucous membranes, nervous disorders, reproductive failure. *Deficiency unlikely*
B₁ (Thiamine)	Red meat, whole grains, legumes, yeast products	Carbohydrate metabolism, heart, nervous system, muscles	Weight loss, ataxia, poor reproduction, degeneration of nerves, brain, muscle, heart

continued

Vitamin	Natural source	Essential for	Deficiency causes
B_2 (Riboflavin)	Meat, grass, alfalfa, milk products, whole grains, yeast products, vegetables	Metabolism of fats, proteins and carbohydrate. Cellular respiration	Foetal abnormalities, dermatitis, alopecia, weakness, poor growth, eye degeneration, anaemia, fatty liver
B_6 (Pyridoxine)	Grains, green vegetables, yeast products, meat	Protein metabolism	Hair loss, symmetrical scaly dermatitis of extremities, anaemia, poor reproduction
B_5 (Pantothenic acid)	Liver, grains, legumes, green vegetables, eggs, potatoes, tomatoes	Efficient use of carbohydrates fats and proteins, the nervous system, formation of skin and fur	Loss of pigmentation, fur loss behind ears, appetite loss, foetal death and abnormalities
B_{12} (Cyanocobalamin)	Liver, meat, milk, egg, cheese, fish, coprophagy. *Synthesised by gut bacteria*	Production of red blood cells, normal cell function	Reduced growth, poor feed utilisation, rough coat, dermatitis, anaemia. *Deficiency rare providing that the rat has not got a gut disorder or is on antibiotics*
D_3 (Cholecalciferol)	Meat, liver, dairy products, eggs fish oils *Added to most feeds*	Healthy bones and teeth	Rickets, osteomalacia (softening of bones in an adult), poor growth and reproduction
E (alpha-tocopherol)	Whole grain and wheat germ, leafy vegetables, grass, alfalfa *Added to most feeds*	Fertility, healthy red blood cells	Foetal reabsorbtion testicular degeneration, muscular degeneration, fragile red cells.
H (Biotin)	Egg yolk, liver, whole grains, green vegetables, coprophagy. *Supplied by gut bacteria*	Aids the synthesis of fats and the utilisation of proteins and carbohydrates	Fur loss, poor growth, skin cracking, rough hair coat. *Deficiency rare providing the rat has not got a gut disorder or is on antibiotics*

continued

Vitamin	Natural source	Essential for	Deficiency causes
K_3 (Menadione)	Green vegetables, cheese, egg yolks, liver, coprophagy. *Most supplied by gut bacteria*	Synthesis of prothrombin for blood clotting. *Warfarin resistant rats require more*	Increased blood clotting times, haemorrhages, anaemia. *Blue group rats may have increased requirement*
Choline	Egg yolk, meat, grains	Synthesis of nucleic acids, nervous system function	Nervous disorders, fatty liver followed by cirrhosis and liver failure. *Deficiency unlikely*
Folates B_9	Liver, meat, low amounts in green vegetables, coprophagy. *Most supplied by gut bacteria*	Red blood cell formation, formation of proteins and nucleic acids	Fur loss, retarded growth. *Deficiency unlikely providing the rat has not got a gut disorder or is on antibiotics*
Niacin (nicotinic acid)	Meat, fish, legumes, eggs nuts	Protein and carbohydrate metabolism	Dermatitis and fur loss, CNS degeneration

Table B – Minerals

Mineral	Natural source	Essential for	Deficiency causes
Calcium	Dairy products, whole grains, green leafy vegetables, egg yolk, legumes, nuts, bones	Healthy bones and teeth, blood clotting, muscle, heart and nerve action, lactation	Rickets, osteoporosis and osteomalacia, poor growth, haemorrhage. *Correct balance with phosphorus and vitamin D essential*
Phosphorus	Dairy products, whole grains, egg yolks, legumes, nuts, bones	As above plus absorption of glucose and transport of fats	Rickets, osteoporosis and osteomalacia
Magnesium	Dairy products, whole grains, egg yolks, legumes, nuts, bones	Healthy teeth, bones, circulation, CNS, heart	Reddening of skin, followed by sores then muscular spasms, convulsions. During pregnancy stillbirths and abnormalities

continued

Mineral	Natural source	Essential for	Deficiency causes
Copper	Liver, meat, sea food, whole grains, legumes, nuts, raisins	Manufacture of keratin for fur, nails etc, iron absorption. Manufacture of coat pigments	Loss of pigmentation especially around the eyes, fur loss, anaemia, neurological abnormalities in severe cases. *Slight deficiency common*
Zinc	Galvanised cage bars!, liver, sea food, eggs, milk, whole grains	Important for many metabolic functions, insulin storage, recovery from infection	Poor growth, thickening of the skin, fur loss, poor wound healing, testicular degeneration
Iron	Liver, meat, egg yolk, whole grains, green leafy vegetables, legumes, nuts	Haemoglobin formation	Anaemia, poor weight gain
Iodine	Seafood, iodised salt	Normal growth, thyroid function and reproduction	Enlarged thyroid, goitre, stillbirths
Cobalt	Absorbed as vitamin B_{12}	Essential for red cell formation	Anaemia
Manganese	Whole grains, legumes, nuts, vegetables, fruit	Many metabolic functions	Poor growth and bone formation, abortions, deformed young, delayed oestrus, reduced ovulation
Selenium*	Seafoods, meats, whole grains (not ones grown in Europe), nuts	Vitamin E absorption, normal cell function	Poor growth and fertility, poor skin and fur health. Possibly increased tumour incidence. Slight deficiency may be common in Europe and UK
Chromium	Meat (not fish), whole grains, molasses, black treacle, and unrefined brown sugar	Glucose metabolism, growth	Raised blood and urine glucose, decreased weight gain and life span. *Severe diabetes does not develop*

*Selenium deficiency is probably quite common in Europe and the UK because our soils are deficient in this element.

5 CHOOSING A VET FOR RATS

ANGELA HORN

Although many aspects of veterinary care will be the same for all mammals, there are certain areas where rats need special consideration. Finding a vet who is experienced in treating rats, or who is at least prepared to read up on it if they are not, can make a real difference in these cases. An experienced vet should know about rat-specific illnesses such as respiratory disease, for example, or that the rat's faster metabolism can mean that it needs a higher dosage of drugs relative to its bodyweight. Some surgical techniques, such as castration, are different from those for other species, so it is vital that the rat is not treated simply as a smaller version of a cat!

So, how does one find a rat-friendly vet? Other rat owners may be able to recommend vets they have used. This is a good starting point, but it does not guarantee that those vets are particularly experienced with rats; just that another rat owner has been pleased with their approach. Many of us are not in a position to assess whether our vet gave the best possible treatment or not, so often all we can comment on is whether the vet seemed to handle our pets with care.

Whether you first heard of a vet through a recommendation, or through the *Yellow Pages* etc, I would recommend finding out a little more before taking your rats to them. Telephone the surgery and talk to the receptionist or veterinary nurse first of all. Ask if:

1. The practice sees many rats?
2. Is there a vet who has a special interest in rodents (sometimes known as 'small furries')?
3. If your rats ever need an operation, could they do it?
4. Do they use Isoflurane anaesthesia?

Isoflurane is a very gentle and effective modern anaesthetic gas. It is safer for small mammals than injected anaesthetics and older inhaled anaesthetics such as halothane. Although there are always risks associated with an anaesthetic, they are rare with isoflurane, and vets who have used it, swear by it. Vets who have not used it tend to say that the skill of the anaesthetist is more important than the drug used. Isoflurane is more expensive than the alternatives, and so is not available in all surgeries. Personally I would not risk having a rat operated on using any other drug.

Beware of anyone who says 'We don't usually operate on rodents as they probably wouldn't survive the anaesthetic' – this is a sure sign that they lack experience with rats.

If your rat needs surgery, ask for a quote beforehand. It is reasonable for them to charge the same prices as they would for cats: it takes at least as long to operate on a rat after all. Most of us would be horrified if someone said 'Don't spend much money on treatment, it's only a RAT.' If we want vets to treat rats with the same care and respect afforded to cats and dogs we need to treat vets with respect too, and pay the going rate for their time! If you are having financial difficulties, some surgeries will allow you to pay by instalments.

Some vets reduce their charges for rats, because they worry that the owner will not be able to afford (or be willing to pay) the full rate. In such surgeries, the partners are effectively subsidising rat owners out of their own pay. However, if the quote you are given seems excessive, it may be that the vet really does not want to do the work!

I hope that these considerations will help you find a vet who is genuinely interested in treating rats. However, the final test is how you feel about the vet. Do you like the way they handle your rats? Do you feel able to ask them about their proposed treatments? Are your questions answered, or are your concerns brushed aside? You and your vet will be partners in your animals' healthcare; you need to respect each other!

6 PRE- AND POST-OPERATIVE CARE

VERONICA SIMMONS

There is always some risk with surgery in any animal and it is sensible to find a vet who is used to operating on rats if your rat needs an operation. Two of the commonest procedures which are usually worthwhile are the removal of benign mammary tumours (mammary fibroadenomas and lipomas) and castration of bucks which have become unacceptably aggressive to their cage mates and owners. It is important that a rat undergoing surgery is not suffering from any respiratory illness.

You may be advised to starve the rat overnight before the operation, as you would a dog or cat, but this is not necessary or advisable. Rats cannot vomit and a starved or dehydrated animal is less likely to stand up to the stress of surgery well. In any case, if rats are hungry they will eat their own faeces or bedding.

When you collect the rat after its operation it should be fully conscious. Vets who use gaseous anaesthetics, such as isoflurane, seem to have a greater success rate than those who use injectable ones. Rats take longer to recover from the latter and need more careful nursing. It also helps if the vet supports the rat during the operation with subcutaneous fluids and a heating pad. If your rat seems a bit woozy when you collect it, make sure that it is turned every two hours or so to prevent fluid building up in the lungs, which can lead to pneumonia.

It is important to keep the patient warm but not overheated. Put the rat in a plastic bottomed cage with plenty of clean soft paper, Vetbed or towelling rather than sawdust; you do not want it to inhale sawdust. Give it a box for cover and keep it warm, but not hot, by placing a heating pad on the lowest setting under part of the cage (the rat should be able to get away from the heat if he wants). The fleece covered heating pads designed for human aches and pains are ideal for this. If you haven't got one of these you can use an under floor heater designed for reptiles or a covered hot water bottle. Hot water bottles lose heat however and will require refilling. Give the patient plenty of fluids and encourage it to eat with a variety of titbits. Moist foods are best such as grapes, peas, oat cereal or wholemeal bread mixed with a little milk or water, baby foods and Complan. Foods high in protein are valuable after surgery.

Some vets put an Elizabethan collar on a rat after surgery to stop it pulling out its stitches but these are not suitable for short legged animals. A cervical collar, as described in *Rat Health Care* by Debbie Ducommun, enables the rat to eat and drink without being able to reach its wound. If you and the rat are lucky, your vet will have done subcuticular stitches which the rat cannot get at and which dissolve with time. If the worst happens and the rat rips out its stitches after the operation, don't panic. Rat skin heals quickly and if the operation was for something superficial like a mammary tumour more stitches and another anaesthetic may do more harm than good. However it would be wise to let the vet assess this. If your rat appears to be in pain or has no appetite seek veterinary advice because most rats usually recover quickly. Make sure that the bedding and wound are kept clean.

You may be advised to keep the patient away from its cage mates for a week or more but if the rat is healing well after one or two days it will probably feel all the better for being with its friends, particularly if it is a doe. Just keep the cage extra clean. The rehabilitation of aggressive bucks is more tricky because it takes two or three weeks for the calming effects of castration to be noticeable. In theory neutered bucks should be able to live with bucks or does eventually, but in practice they are generally happier with does.

Bibliography

The Biology and Medicine of Rabbits and Rodents, 4th edn, eds J. E. Harkness and J. E. Wagner, 1995 Williams and Watkins

Common Tumours in the Rat, A. Storey, 1999 Supplement to *Pro-Rat-a* **112**

Diseases of Small Domestic Rodents, V. C. G. Richardson, 1997 Blackwell Science

Experimental and Surgical Technique in the Rat, 2nd edn, H. B. Waynforth and P. A. Flecknell, 1992 Academic Press

Foot and Mouth Disease in the Brown Rat, Maureen Capel-Edwards, 1970 *Journal of Comparative Pathology,* **80**, 543-548

The Genetics of the Norway Rat, R. Robinson, 1965 Pergamon Press

Handbook of Rodent and Rabbit Medicine, eds K. Laber-Laird, M. M. Swindle and P. Flecknell, 1996 Pergamon Press

The Laboratory Rat, Vol 1, eds H. J. Baker, J. Russell Lindsey and S. H. Weisbroth, 1979, Academic Press

Mycoplasmal Respiratory Disease in Rats and Mice, A. Storey, 1997, *Pro-Rat-a* **100** pp 18-21. Also www.nfrs.org

Pathology of Laboratory Rodents and Rabbits, 2nd edn, D. Percy and S. W. Barthold, 2001. Iowa State University Press, Ames

Rat Health Care, Debbie Ducommun, The Rat Fan Club

There are also many other snippets of information both from fanciers and *Pro-Rat-a*. Of particular help have been articles by Rachel Rodham, Debbie Ducommun, Claire Jordan, Peter Gregory, Ed Friedlander, Lucy Whitcombe, Veronica Simmons, Estelle Sandford, Joan Branton, Sara Handley and Alison Campbell.